THE UNITED NATIONS
AND HOW IT WORKS

The United Nations and How It Works

REVISED EDITION

David Cushman Coyle

WITH AN INTRODUCTION BY Dr. Hernane Tavares de Sá

Columbia University Press
NEW YORK AND LONDON

To my wife
DORIS PORTER COYLE
with deep appreciation
for many hours of research
and for the benefit
of her judgment and editorial help
in the writing of this book

CONTENTS

INTRODUCTION

The human side of the work of the United Nations—perhaps the most important aspect of an organization whose Charter was proclaimed in the name of the peoples of the world—is not always brought out in the day-to-day reports of its activities.

This book by David Cushman Coyle is all the more to be commended because it tells the UN story from the "ground level" approach and in terms of its effect on us, or people like us.

It is not a record of continuing success. What is constant, however, is the unflagging effort to resolve for the common good problems which touch our lives at so many key points—food, shelter, livelihood, and, above all, the desire to live in peace and freedom.

The opinions expressed in this book are, of course, the author's own, but the impression he leaves with the reader is one that most will agree parallels the thought recently expressed by the Secretary-General of the United Nations: "No matter how deep the shadows may be, how sharp the conflicts, how tense the mistrust . . . we are not permitted to forget that we have too much in common, too great a sharing of interests and too much that we might lose together . . . ever to weaken our efforts to surmount the difficulties and not to turn the simple human values, which are our common heritage, into the firm foundation on which we may unite our strength and live together in peace."

This new and revised edition has been published in cooperation with the Office of Public Information of the United Nations.

HERNANE TAVARES DE SÁ
United Nations Under-Secretary for
Public Information

FOREWORD

In the spring of 1945 World War II was plainly drawing to a close. Millions of people had died in that war; millions more were homeless, hungry, and cold. The people of the whole world longed for a lasting peace. The victims of war devastation, and hundreds of millions who suffered grinding poverty even in peacetime, longed also for an escape from poverty, hunger, and disease. All over the world, too, wherever people lived under foreign domination or home-grown oppression, there was a growing demand for freedom and justice.

These deep desires for peace and for better conditions of life were joined in the great conference at San Francisco in the spring of 1945, when the nations combined their efforts in the organization of the United Nations.

The UN was organized to deal with the quarrels between nations that might lead to war. At the same time, the UN and its many working agencies have been helping the member nations in the agelong fight against human misery, injustice, and oppression.

The main purposes of the United Nations are not in conflict. It is clear that peace is necessary if the people of the world are to be free and prosperous. But peace does not come by accident; it has to be built by many kinds of action working together to provide for collective security and to remove the causes of war. United efforts to build a more prosperous world by cooperation among people of different nations and races may also help to lay the foundations for a lasting peace. People who work together against the hostile forces of nature often become friends. And finally, the united pressure of world opinion in support of human rights will in time help to reduce some of the causes of war among the peoples of the world.

The material works of the UN agencies—helping to build dams, to kill mosquitoes, to teach people to read—and its spiritual works, such as framing the Universal Dec-laration of Human Rights, may be fully as important for peace as the great conferences and the search for a way to control the atom.

World-wide struggles against the hostile forces of nature are easily understood by millions of people who feel baffled by the harder problems of quarreling human nature. These material works of the UN therefore serve as a background for the UN efforts to hold the conflicts of human nature below the explosion point. The UN does not pretend that it can surely persuade or force all men to work together in harmony all the time. But it can help to bring world opinion to bear on many kinds of disputes that if left to fester between enemies might break out into deadly war.

The United Nations can talk about the rights of man, and by such talk can put moral pressure on nations where people are treated in ways that the world regards as wrong. The United Nations can take an interest in colonial peoples and in their progress toward independence or self-government—an interest that the governing powers cannot lightly brush aside.

The United Nations has been able to stop or to prevent several wars since 1945, notably in Palestine and Kashmir. In Korea the UN forces beat back the aggression. There can be, of course, no absolute guarantee that any organization on earth could surely prevent a third great war and the possible suicide of the human race. But much can be done to make that doom less likely; and much of it is being done in the United Nations.

In the United Nations, the human race is brought together, with all its virtues and faults, its wisdom and folly, and its good and ill will. This is not a world government. This is a world meeting to talk over the pressing dangers of our times and to hunt for the way to prosperity and world peace. It cannot rule the world by making and enforcing a world law with planes and atom bombs. But it can bring to bear the moral weight of world opinion. The recommendations of the Assembly of the United Nations may be all the more effective because they do not demand obedience but only ask a decent respect for the opinions of mankind.

The organization of the United Nations and how it operates are described at some length in Chapter 11. At this point it will be enough to describe briefly the main features of the UN organization.

At the center is the General Assembly, where every member nation is represented and has one vote. No nation has a veto power in the General Assembly.

The Security Council has eleven members. Five of these are the permanent members: Britain, China, France, the Union of Soviet Socialist Republics, and the United States of America. In voting on measures classed as "substantive" rather than "procedural," a motion cannot in most cases pass unless all the five permanent members vote for it. That is, each of these nations has a "veto." The difference between substantive and procedural is supposed to be related to the difference between actions on the merits of a question and actions affecting only the internal arrangements of the Council's work, but there naturally are likely to be disputes as to how a particular question is to be classified.

The six nonpermanent members of the Security Council are elected by the General Assembly for two-year terms, and do not have the veto power.

The International Court of Justice is made up of fifteen judges elected by the General Assembly and the Security Council.

The Economic and Social Council (ECOSOC) consists of the representatives of eighteen member states chosen by the General Assembly. This Council helps to coordinate the activities of many affiliated agencies dealing with international cooperation in all kinds of work from fighting epidemics to carrying the international mails. Nongovernmental organizations are often consulted by ECOSOC on questions with which they are concerned.

The Trusteeship Council supervises the administration of various territories that are governed by certain Powers as trustees. The Council considers reports and petitions and makes periodic visits to inspect the territories.

A list of the principal UN agencies, with their abbreviations, is given in Appendix A. The Charter, adopted in San Franciso in 1945 to be the Constitution of the United Nations, is given in full in Appendix B. The list of member states is given in Appendix C.

THE GRASS ROOTS

The United Nations Headquarters in New York is a strange place where the top of the organized human race breaks through the surface. In the gallery of the Assembly you can listen to a speaker talking in a foreign tongue. Or you can put on the earphones and hear the translator giving the speech in your own language, and yet it may not sound real.

It is often real enough, however, for this is the point of contact where contending nations can grind ponderously together, striving to get what they want without the fearful costs of military war. The grinding is real, though the words themselves may seem obscure. These people are talking about something. There must be more here than meets the eye.

There is more than meets the eye. Behind the delegates are not only their nations, each with its own interests and strategy. There is also the UN itself, with its Charter and institutions, to muster the moral and material forces of mankind. The UN rests on the faith and hope of the millions of people who look to it to take their part against the danger of war and the troubles of peace. And down in the grass roots of the world, where millions of people have never learned to read or write, these people are seeing the ground-level workings of the United Nations.

Down in the grass roots the UN is building its foundations by helping people to get more to eat, and to be free of epidemic diseases, and to start hoping for a better future. The people who see that side of it soon come to understand what it means.

11

The Better Future

Most of the people on earth are not as well off as the people of the Western world. Children born in Southeast Asia, for instance, can expect to live about thirty years. In the United States, as of 1957, the average lifetime for men was 66.3 years and for women 72.5 years. In Norway it is several years longer. These long average lifetimes reflect comparative freedom from disease, ignorance, and poverty.

A hundred years ago the people in Western countries died young. Since then there have been changes, caused mainly by science and invention. These changes prove that many of the age-old troubles of mankind can now be reduced to small proportions or even totally abolished. All over the world those who still suffer show signs of discontent. They feel something new in the air, as if there might be an escape from their troubles, if they could only find it.

In the lands where people suffer from unnecessary ignorance, poverty, and disease, the United Nations brings a new hope. If there is time, and if the atom does not first wipe out civilization, the work of the UN among the grass roots may yet save the human race from despair.

Rice

About half the people in the world live mostly on rice. Most of the rice-eating people are poor. Rice, therefore, is a key to the main problem of survival in many overcrowded areas around the world.

Different countries have different systems for growing rice, some better than others. And there are two main kinds of rice, *japonica* and *indica*. Japonica rice in Japan yields about three times as much per acre as indica in India, but India cannot adopt japonica because it is a temperate-zone plant. The indica is suited to the tropics. This is a case for hybrids, some of which may combine the high yields of japonica with indica's ability to stand the tropical climate.

The Government of India is host to a Rice Research Station, sponsored by the UN Food and Agriculture Organization (FAO) and ten other Asian countries. The program consists of crossing varieties of japonica and

12

indica and selecting the hybrids that can be used in various countries. No one standard hybrid can be expected to turn out best for all climates and methods of cultivation.

In course of time the traditional methods of rice growing will be studied and improved. There are great differences in the rice yield per acre in various countries. Japan produces 2,350 pounds of rice per acre, while the U.S.A. rice fields yield only 1,390 pounds per acre. Both countries plant japonica rice, but in Japan where land is scarce, more labor is put into the acre. The United States has plenty of rice land and labor is costly, so the planters use machines. They get a lower yield per acre but at a low cost per ton. Both methods are generally well suited to the conditions in which they are used, but they are not necessarily as efficient as they might become with more international exchange of information.

Farmers are slower in changing their methods of cultivation than they are in accepting new kinds of seed. This is a reason for the urgency of the hybridization project. Hybrid corn (maize) has already shown such increases over the yields of ordinary corn that it is rapidly becoming universal. In view of the great differences in yields between different strains of rice, the chances for a revolutionary improvement in most of the rice-growing countries are encouraging.

At the present stage, the UN work in rice breeding is unknown to the millions of people who may benefit from it. But it is not a high theory that will remain forever in the minds of learned technicians. As the new seeds are introduced the people will see the exciting change in their own lives, when the same land and the same year's labor will bring forth twice as much to eat. For people who are almost always hungry, that will seem like something to build a new world upon.

As a matter of fact, these simple grass-roots developments are usually far more profitable than ordinary business or industrial enterprises. An expenditure of half a million dollars in one of these programs can easily add a hundrd million dollars' worth to the total output of a country. This is one reason why a developing country can afford to contribute most of the cost of such projects, except for what has to be paid in foreign money. As development goes on beyond the simplest improvements in agriculture and public health, the rate of return comes down to the usual commerical and industrial percentages and finance becomes a more crucial factor. But at the start, a well-managed grass-roots program can be a strong stimulus to progress not only by encouraging the people but also by giving them a quick increase of income. This is an advantage that the UN has over the old League of Nations. Thirty years ago there were few chances to start such high-profit grass-roots projects, chiefly because the quick and cheap cures for the great debilitating diseases had not yet been invented.

Airways

One of the peculiarities of modern technology is that some of the wildest countries in the world can make immediate use of the most complex inventions. The airplane and radio, because they can jump over deserts and mountains, are in great demand where hard traveling conditions have always been an obstacle to progress. Iran, the ancient country of Persia, although it has one of the oldest civilizations in the world, also has a great amount of undeveloped country cut up by deserts and mountains. Iran is about as big as France, Italy, Spain, and Norway combined, but it has only about one-tenth as many people.

The Government of Iran therefore asked the UN for technical advice on the expansion of its airways. The International Civil Aviation Organization, one of the UN specialized agencies, sent experts to advise the Iranian airways on the improvement of their service and to help the government Department of Civil Aviation to train ground crews. Classes were organized for the study of air traffic control and radio techniques, supplemented by on-the-job training.

The experts composing the first ICAO mission included four from the Netherlands, two from Norway, one from Britain, and one refugee without a country. ICAO also provided fellowships for Iranians to study aeronautical engineering and electronics abroad. In 1955 Iran started its first regular domestic airmail service after three years' work by a UN postal mission.

In Ethiopia an aviation school was established at Addis Ababa, with instructors supplied by ICAO. Ethiopia now has a network of weather-reporting stations, and the school is turning out Ethiopian mechanics to service the planes of the Ethiopian Air Lines.

In Mexico City the Mexican Government in cooperation with ICAO has set up a school for training ground crews and pilots, which in 1960 had about two hundred students from all parts of Latin America.

Canalboats

Canals, rivers, and lakes have always been natural highways in the flat part of the world, and millions of people live their lives in boats on the quiet inland waterways. In East Pakistan, for instance, there are some millions of boats, from rowboats to sailing sampans, godowns —tall warehouses on rafts—and steamers and motor craft. Many of the types are ancient, and they operate with a lavish use of cheap labor. Some of the great barges are rowed with sweeps that take nine men to an oar. But progress means a rising standard of living for poor men. No man can earn a good living pulling one-ninth of an oar. Gradually as standards and wages rise, workers must shift to more profitable jobs. Motors have to push or drag the heavy barges even on the ancient Ganges and Brahmaputra.

The Government of Pakistan turned to the United Nations for help in modernizing its inland water transport. Pakistan was not the only country with inland waterway problems, for in most of the Far East half the people live in the great river deltas and depend on water highways. One of the results of the inquiries from Asia was the organization of the Inland Water Transport Tour, an expedition of Asian experts to view the operation of waterways in other parts of the world. Members of the tour came from Burma, India, Indonesia, Pakistan, Thailand, and Vietnam. The group started by visiting Thailand, Burma, Pakistan, and India, so as to learn about one another's problems.

The Asians then proceeded to Europe, where they visited shipyards and waterways in France, Germany, and the Netherlands. They inspected new types of boats and tugs in England and Scotland. Going on to the United States, they studied traffic and equipment on the Ohio and Mississippi and along the intracoastal canals.

The members of the tour discussed the problems of water transport with experts in the countries they visited, comparing steam and diesel engines, push-towing and pull-towing, and self-propelled barges. They studied riveted and welded barges, aluminum barges, tankers and refrigerated barges, and methods of mechanical loading and unloading. The information that they collected had to be digested and sorted out to find what might be useful in Asia. The value of labor-saving in any country depends on the going rate of wages. Wages have to rise gradually as modern methods are introduced and jobs open up where the workers can earn the higher wages. If high-powered machinery is brought in too fast, it does not make the country richer. On the contrary, business is dislocated by throwing men out of work. Another limitation is the cost of foreign machinery, which has to be paid in dollars or some other foreign money. The trade balance of the country can stand just so much.

If technical improvements are introduced at the proper rate of speed, allowing time for the displaced workers to get new jobs and for the foreign-exchange costs to be covered by increased exports, progress will go along smoothly. The old League of Nations was well aware of the limitations on the proper rate of progress, and the United Nations agencies are even better aware of it. This is a part of the problem of digesting foreign information which was one of the main jobs of the members of the Inland Water Transport Tour. They returned to their countries prepared, not to imitate what they had seen in the West, but to do their own work with a wider background of experience to stimulate their invention.

As a result many improvements have been introduced. Inland Water Transport Boards have been set up, and conferences are held regularly to stimulate progress in the equipment and management of water traffic.

Fish Farming

Indonesia, formerly the Dutch East Indies, ranks as "underdeveloped" in Western science and technology. But it was a highly civilized country when the United States was a thin line of colonial settlements along the Atlantic shore, and when a Javanese princess married the Dutch Dr. Staats and migrated with him to the New World to become ancestress of some of the proudest families of New York.

The Indonesian civilization developed not only the arts but also some kinds of technical knowledge that are superior to any similar techniques in other parts of the world.

One of these ancient Indonesian techniques is fish farming. When the water is turned into the rice fields the farmers stock them with baby carp from the breeding ponds. The carp and rice grow up together for about three months. By the time the fields are drained the fish are the size of large sardines and ready to eat.

The UN has arranged for students from as far away as Haiti and Israel to study fish farming in Indonesia in order to help in developing similar fish supplies for their own countries.

Land Reform

In most of the countries where the farmers are poor and uneducated the ownership of farm lands is unsatisfactory. The most common source of discontent is "landlordism." The land is owned in large tracts by landlords who rent it out to the cultivators at exorbitant rents, running as high as three-fourths of the crop. The farmers naturally hate the landlords and long for the day when they themselves can own the land. The cure of these evils is not simple, and the farmers may be fooled by cruel and dishonest promises.

The most obvious way for enraged farmers to get rid of their rent burdens might seem to be to liquidate the landlords and take over the land. The drawback is that such violent methods would not protect the farmers from the kind of government that would go with them. After the farmer got possession of his land, he might find that the taxes, the forced deliveries to the government, and the days of forced labor on government work, would add up to a heavier burden than before.

The UN had a Conference on Natural Resources in 1949, where most of the delegates crowded into the meetings on land reform. They discussed the problems of their various countries and learned how complex the subject can be.

The General Assembly therefore passed a resolution

in 1950 asking the Secretary-General and the FAO to study the problems of landholding. In 1951 the Economic and Social Council discussed the Secretary-General's report, and recommended to the member governments that they take up land reform "in the interest of the landless, small, and medium farmers." The United States sponsored a World Conference, and many countries started programs to improve the conditions of land ownership.

One of the most successful land distribution programs so far has been in Japan, where the Occupation authorities directed the purchase of five million acres from landlords. The land was sold to the tenants at fair prices and the payments were spread over thirty years with an interest rate of only 3.2 per cent. The farmers had a good bargain and they knew it.

At the same time, the landlords, instead of being liquidated, came out with valuable government bonds. Reports from Japan indicate that the Japanese people are well pleased with the effects of the land distribution.

Dr. Bennett, the late head of the United States Point Four Program, offered the following general principles for a just and equitable agricultural system:

> First, the farmer must be able to own land, or to use the land he tills under fair conditions and terms of tenure. Second, the farmer must have access to credit on reasonable terms to enable him to farm efficiently, whether as owner or tenant. Third, he must have access to knowledge and techniques that will make his efforts productive and profitable to him and to society.

Techniques have been developed through which the success of the farmer on his land can be hastened and rendered more secure. The system of "supervised credit," for instance, offers the farmer enough credit to buy machinery, fertilizer, and high-grade seed, on his agreement to follow a plan of operations worked out with a technical adviser. Ordinarily the result is an increase in production and income that appears almost miraculous.

The Economic and Social Council in 1957 suggested that governments undertake studies of the effects of land-reform measures on production, living standards, and economic and social development. It also called attention to the fact that technical advice could be obtained from the UN and various specialized agencies.

In 1958 the Council suggested the establishment of regional research and training centers to study problems of land tenure and land use and invited FAO and other appropriate agencies to cooperate in this work.

The Agencies

The UN work at the grass roots is carried on by several agencies that deal with the basic material enemies of man—hunger, disease, and poverty.

Hunger is the special problem of the Food and Agriculture Organization (FAO), which was started in 1943 at a conference of national representatives in Hot Springs, Virginia. FAO has its own constitution and membership; not all FAO members belong to the UN. It has its own income derived from dues paid by the members, and its own governing body, the FAO Conference, which meets every two years. FAO is one of the specialized agencies affiliated with the UN through an agreement with the Economic and Social Council, approved by the UN General Assembly.

FAO sends experts to help countries that want technical advice on how to grow more food and other crops, how to control pests and plant and animal diseases, how to protect food in storage, and in general how to increase the yield of farms, fisheries, and forests. For example, FAO has been successfully fighting rinderpest, a disease that before 1946 killed about two million cattle a year. As a result of FAO's efforts rinderpest is now being rapidly controlled throughout the world by large-scale vaccination. FAO is also pushing the breeding of special strains of livestock that will stand unfavorable conditions, the improved feeding of livestock and poultry in the underdeveloped areas, and the conservation and improvement of ranges and natural grasslands.

FAO advises on soil conservation and the use of fertilizers. It provides fellowships for technicians to study in foreign countries where they can learn techniques that they can use at home. It also publishes technical yearbooks and other material useful in agriculture, forestry, and fisheries.

FAO illustrates an important difference between the

League of Nations technical agencies and those of the United Nations. A technical agency commonly does three kinds of work: (1) It is a clearinghouse of scientific information through which technical papers are exchanged among scientists of member nations. (2) It promotes standardized legal arrangements among the nations in connection with its specialty. Both these types of work were done by the League agencies and are now carried on by those connected with the UN. (3) It provides technical assistance, of which there was almost none under the League.

Since it is technical assistance that brings the UN into direct contact with millions of people, this difference from the old League is important. In this respect the UN has broader foundations than the League; this may make the difference between life and death for the UN.

The World Health Organization was started by a conference in New York in July, 1946, where representatives of sixty-one countries set up an Interim Commission to work on international health. The permanent organization came into being on April 7, 1948, when twenty-six members had ratified its Constitution. April 7 is now celebrated all over the world as World Health Day.

Even before 1948 the Interim Commission had begun to show what an international organization could do. Egypt was suddenly attacked by an epidemic of cholera in September, 1947. The Commission straightway mustered the cholera experts of the world, and the necessary materials for them to work with. By the end of December the epidemic was wiped out.

WHO is a specialized agency which advises member countries on public health and the control of disease. It makes war on the widespread plagues such as malaria, tuberculosis, yaws, and syphilis, and on less common diseases including leprosy, typhus, polio, diphtheria, and bilharziasis.

In 1955 WHO undertook a world-wide campaign to wipe malaria from the face of the earth, a campaign that has been called "the greatest challenge in the history of humanity's fight for health." One of the most important discoveries of this century is the simple fact that a mosquito that has bitten a malaria patient will rest on the nearest wall to digest the meal, so if the inside walls of the houses

are sprayed with DDT, the disease-carrying mosquitoes
will get it on their feet and die. By the end of 1959 almost
280 million people had been reached with some malaria
protection, out of some 1.4 billion who live in malarial
country.

WHO had two emergency jobs in Morocco in 1959-60.
First, in November, 1959, it appeared that ten thousand
Moroccans were threatened with a paralysis caused by a
mineral oil that had been mixed with their cooking oil.
WHO and other agencies helped the government to organize treatment, relief, and retraining of the paralyzed
victims.

Then the city of Agadir was devastated on the last day
of February and first of March, 1960, by two earthquakes,
a tidal wave, and fires, with widespread loss of life and
property. WHO, at the government's request, sent a con-
sultant to aid in organizing health services in the city.

In some fields of health such as the relation between
health and food, WHO overlaps the work of FAO and
they operate together.

Another agency that often works in close contact with
great numbers of people is the International Labor Organization. ILO was founded in 1919 as a self-governing
institution associated with the League of Nations. It is
now a specialized agency affiliated with the UN.

The annual Conference of the ILO promotes laws for
the protection of wage earners by proposing international
agreements which the delegates are obligated to take home
and submit to their governments for ratification. A government that ratifies one of these agreements binds itself
to report each year on what progress it is making toward
passing the laws called for in the agreement. From 1919
to May, 1960, ILO sent out 114 agreements and received
notice of nearly 2,000 ratifications.

In March, 1956, ILO appointed a committee to study
automation, and its Director-General devoted most of
his 1957 report to that subject. The principal conclusions
were that automation and related technological advances
make it possible to produce many things that could not be
produced before, and that they offer possibilities of higher
living standards. Although they require shifting many
workers to new jobs, they need not cause permanent
unemployment if other conditions are adjusted to keep
abreast of the necessary changes. In other words, if

incomes are so distributed among the people that con-
sumers can buy all the increased production, the markets
will not glut and employment will continue. This refers to
the general principle, already well recognized, that prosperity depends on a sufficiently high rate of total
expenditure, private and governmental.

Important among ILO activities of 1959–60 was the
decision to establish an International Institute of Labor
Studies at Geneva, to bring together labor specialists from
different countries for study and discussion of social and
economic questions. The Institute will serve as an advance
staff college in the field of labor policy, dealing with
matters of special interest to the ILO.

The United Nations International Children's Emergency
Fund (UNICEF) was created by the General Assembly in
1946. UNRRA, the UN Relief and Rehabilitation Administration, which had been set up to relieve victims of
war devastation, was closing its work in 1946, and
UNICEF took over the relief of children who still needed
help. UNICEF is not supported by the UN budget, but by
voluntary contributions from governments and individuals
—including the sale of the widely used UNICEF Christmas
cards.

UNICEF specializes in the supply of medicines, food,
and equipment for maternal and child welfare services;
control of diseases specially affecting children; child
nutrition; and relief of children in earthquakes, floods,
famines, and volcanic eruptions. Its work overlaps WHO
and FAO in many places and the organizations work
together, each supplying what it can do best.

Two of the most important present jobs at UNICEF
are its campaigns against yaws and tuberculosis.

Yaws is a disease of hot damp climates. Yaws makes
masses of open sores. It is extremely contagious, and
especially afflicts children. Few die of yaws, but many
become helpless cripples and a lifelong burden on their
relatives.

Yaws can be cured with one dose of penicillin costing
fifteen cents.

Indonesia, for example, as soon as it became an
independent nation, asked the UN to help in a war
against yaws. There were estimated to be 10,000,000
cases in the country when the job was undertaken in
1950. UNICEF gave the material and WHO sent medical

experts to train Indonesian workers. Indonesia supplied buildings, workers, and the equipment that did not have to come from abroad.

In four years the hundreds of medical teams, trained by WHO and supplied with jeeps and materials from UNICEF, had examined 11,000,000 people and cured 1,300,000 who had yaws. Many villages are now free of yaws; another few years and practically the whole country will be free of it. After that, as time goes on and the cripples die, they will not be replaced by more cripples.

Yaws has been practially wiped out in Haiti, and campaigns are going on in more than twenty-five other countries. The demand for penicillin—which is also used against syphilis, a close cousin of yaws—has been out-running the supply, so UNICEF and the UN Technical Assistance Administration have helped to build new antibiotics plants in India, Chile, and Yugoslavia.

By the end of 1959, in the countries where UNICEF was aiding campaigns against yaws, over 75,000,000 persons had been examined and over 27,000,000 treated, half of them mothers and children. More than half of the people in areas where yaws is a common disease had been covered.

Tuberculosis is another mass plague that strikes most often where living conditions are poor, and most often strikes children and young people. In India, for instance, TB kills about half a million people a year. It is also a great cause of poverty because it is a slow killer. People waste away and cannot work to support themselves.

In the crowded countries with low standards of living, there is no present chance to send the TB patients to hospitals for treatment. But there is one thing that can be done quickly, and that is to vaccinate the children who have not yet caught the disease.

The vaccine, known as BCG, discovered in France fifty years ago, has been developed and tested on a large scale by the Scandinavians. In 1948, UNICEF and the Scandinavians joined forces with WHO to put on campaigns in countries that asked for help.

The BCG teams go into a village and test the children for TB. Those who have not been infected are vaccinated. Of those who are vaccinated, about 80 per cent cannot get TB for four or five years, and the other 20 per cent will not have it severely. From then on it is only necessary to vaccinate all newborn babies and keep up the immunity of the others. As the unfortunate ones who were already infected gradually die off, the number of cases and the amount of infection will diminish. Finally, if the country grows rich enough, and if the search for still newer drugs proceeds as expected, the disease can be virtually wiped out.

In the meantime, the operation is extremely profitable. One vaccination costs only about twenty cents, less than the cost of two UNICEF Christmas cards in the UN bookshop. The child who doesn't get TB may grow up and earn his own living instead of being a burden on his family. For twenty cents every four years, the profit to the country is high.

In 1952, UNICEF and WHO launched an experimental campaign against trachoma in Morocco. Trachoma is an eye disease that often causes blindness. Some good results were obtained, but it was evident that a massive attack on the universal plague of flies would be needed, since flies carry the disease. That in turn must depend on widespread health education.

In 1953, when the International Children's Emergency Fund came to the end of its emergency charter, the Fund reported that it had vaccinated 22 million children with BCG, cured 3 million of yaws, protected 12 million from malaria, and so on through a long list. The General Assembly voted unanimously to continue the Fund indefinitely and gave it a new name, the UN Children's Fund. But the initials UNICEF were kept as a trade-mark. To millions of people, the only United Nations they know is UNICEF, the friend of children.

The other principal UN agency working directly at the grass roots is the UN Educational, Scientific, and Cultural Organization (UNESCO), which covers the whole field of education and therefore overlaps all the other agencies. It is entitled to a separate chapter and is described in Chapter 2.

Several important programs aiding the underdeveloped countries to raise their standards of living are being carried on outside the UN. One is the Point Four Program of the United States; another is the Colombo Plan set up by members of the British Commonwealth. There are also numerous private institutions working on special problems, such as the Rockefeller Foundation and the Ford Foundation. The Organization of American States has many specialized agencies for development work, often in close cooperation with the UN agencies. France and the Soviet Union have widespread programs for aiding economic development in various parts of the world.

When the UN agencies are asked to assist a country with technical development, they request the government to arrange that all organizations related to the proposed work be brought into a cooperative plan. An example is the rehabilitation center for cripples at Solo in Java, started by an Indonesian surgeon after the war. In 1954 the UN sent an expert from the United States to visit Solo. As a result of his report the center was built up with the cooperative help of the Indonesian Government, the United Nations, the World Veterans' Foundation, ILO, WHO, and the Directors of the Colombo Plan.

The Expanded Program

The UN Charter recognized that there was a wide demand for economic development, and there was also a growing realization that poverty might be a cause of discontent and of war. In January, 1949, President Truman in his Inaugural Address announced a "bold new program" of economic progress for the less developed countries of the world, later known as Point Four. This announcement aroused such enthusiasm that the UN was able to find support for an effort to increase the work of its own technical assistance agencies.

As a result the Expanded Program of Technical Assistance was adopted. A special account was set up to which the member nations were asked to contribute. In June, 1950, representatives of 54 nations met and pledged the equivalent of $20,000,000 for the first eighteen months of the new program. The United States contributed 60 per cent of this first budget. By 1957 some 84 countries and territories pledged over $31,000,000 for the year's budget, and the United States provided less than half of the total.

The UN and eight related agencies share in the funds available each year to operate jointly the Expanded Program. The UN has its own Technical Assistance Board within the Secretariat to help carry out certain projects. The Board takes care of requests for services that do not come in the field of any other agency, such as general development plans, national income census, town planning, industrial development programs, and land and inland water transport.

The Expanded Program of Technical Assistance in its first ten years sent 8,000 experts to 140 countries and territories, gave 14,000 fellowships for students from less-developed countries to study abroad, and made modest grants of equipment and supplies. Cutting across these classifications are numerous training institutions, seminars, and group study tours. With the aid of the International Atomic Energy Agency and the specialized agencies, the program has been able to respond to requests in nearly all technical fields of work.

To help meet the heavy demand for working administrators, the Assembly in 1958 authorized the Secretary-General to aid governments in borrowing a limited number of experienced operational executives (the so-called OPEX program).

The newest technical assistance agency to be established is the UN Special Fund, inaugurated January 1, 1959, with a budget of $26,000,000 raised by voluntary contributions. It is designed to fill in the gaps between programs of the other agencies in the less-developed countries, particularly the gaps in knowledge of what resources are available, and in the number of trained technicians to undertake their development. The Fund makes arrangements with one of the UN agencies, or a government agency, or sometimes a private contractor, to do the needed work, for which it supplies the money.

As a policy the Fund concentrates on a limited number of fairly large projects. It is particularly interested in providing resource surveys and research to bring out the best uses of special raw materials or other natural resources that may be found in a country. It also helps in establishing technical courses to train the many kinds of engineers, teachers, transport and communications workers, health workers, public administrators, and other skilled people who make up the working body of a modern civilized community. It promotes demonstrations of new methods, including pilot projects. The basic purpose of these programs is to open the way for a more rapid increase of public works and private investment, so that national incomes and standards of living can be raised as fast as possible.

In its first year the Special Fund approved forty-four projects in Africa, Asia, Europe, the Middle East, and the Western Hemisphere. For these projects the Fund's Governing Council allotted $31,900,000. In addition the contributions of the governments assisted were estimated at about $45,000,000.

Material and Moral

What does growing more rice have to do with saving the world from destruction by the H-bomb? Isn't this just playing with pebbles on the beach while an earthquake is sending a tidal wave to wash us all away? It is a dangerous world but it is not as simple as that.

The United Nations has to save the world, if possible, from the H-Bomb in the next few years and from more and worse in the future, from now on as long as civilization endures. In the long run, the human race may survive if people learn not to fear and distrust one another as much as they do now. Organizations to deter military aggression and to build up a secure and harmonious world are necessary. But underlying all that, the issue of life or death is moral, not only among the delegates who discuss and argue in the great conferences but also among the people at home.

When the United Nations sends a team of foreign experts into a village to cure disease or to increase the food supply, they are expected to train local people and work with them. The local contribution to each project is generally many times as large as that of the UN, in terms of labor, equipment, and money. The material purpose of the work is a necessary part of the moral relation that is created among these people. Being a material thing, the reduction of disease or the increase of food can be seen and agreed upon. In the simplest kinds of "development" there is no argument. The people unite to create a new thing and see that it is good. They can shake hands and feel the bond of friendship in a successful common adventure. This is the most fundamental way that good will can come among men of different races, religions, and cultures.

But almost the same kind of activity can create hatreds.

When men work together as master and slave, or as
conqueror and subject people, without mutual respect or
a common purpose, they can build deep-seated hatreds.
There are such hatreds today in most of the world.

When any sort of "project" is undertaken, therefore,
the question has to arise: Is someone out to exploit the
workers in this project for some purpose that they do not
think is good? Is this development program a trap to get
political control of the country? Or are the foreigners
trying to make friends in order to win allies in a war they
are planning? Or do the foreigners simply hope to make
a commercial profit out of the country's development? If
the foreigners have enemies, the enemies will tell the people
that the development projects are a trap. In the long run
the people are going to judge the honesty of the foreign
experts who offer to help them, and they will give them
friendship or hatred accordingly.

There is no dishonesty in wanting to do business with
a growing and prosperous country, if it is honest business
with profit to all concerned in it. There is no dishonesty in
wanting to make friends in order to have allies for the
defense of peace, if the real plan is to defend peace and
not to start an aggressive war. Selfish reasons for helping
in an enterprise are not wrong if they are reasons that
everyone agrees are good.

In fact, good hardheaded reasons for taking part in a
development project are valuable because they are easier
to believe than a professed love of doing good for its own
sake. The foreigners, especially, do well to hunt for hard,
well-understood reasons by which to explain themselves in
order to ward off the natural suspicion with which many
people often regard strangers.

It is natural for an engineer to get satisfaction from
seeing the plans of his brain take form in a stout bridge
that is praised by the people who needed a bridge. It is
natural for a doctor to enjoy winning a tough battle against
a disease. Under the UN flag, men can go on a mission
with men of other nations to do a job that plainly gives
them these creative satisfactions. The same satisfactions
are, to be sure, common among the technicians who work
for the United States Point Four Program or the Colombo
Plan, or for one of the private foundations. But in places
where the people are keenly suspicious of the Great

Powers, the same technicians can go under UN auspices and be more readily accepted.

The best of all reasons for technical assistance is that, carried through in the spirit of good will, it builds the foundations of peace as well as prosperity. At the grass roots of the world, the people may be ignorant of books, but they are wise in human nature. They are suspicious of charity, but they do not miss the meaning of these simple village improvements. In the long run, if the human race is so fortunate as to have a long run, these foundations will bear the growing structure of good will among men.

It is particularly valuable to demonstrate that all the nations can contribute to the pool of knowledge. When, for instance, an expert to fight livestock diseases was needed in Tunisia, one was sent from Ceylon. Columbia has provided a radio specialist for Pakistan. Icelandic fisheries experts have helped to modernize the fishing industries of Ceylon, India, and Turkey. In 1956 India contributed eighty-nine experts for service abroad. The world-wide mutual respect on which peace must finally rest is built up by all such interchanges through which nations that are giving help are also receiving help from others. This growing network of knowledge, with the network of good will which, in the best conditions, grows with it, cannot solve all the fearful problems of a world threatened with destruction, but they are a necessary part of the solution.

The improvement in living conditions where technical assistance has been given by the UN or by the various national and private programs has been notable in many localities and in some places even spectacular. But it is important to remember that so far only scattered lamps of progress have been lighted in a vast gray landscape. This slow total progress is only partially caused by lack of money. Even more it is the effect of scarcity of experts qualified to teach and learn and also free to move to foreign lands. More rapid progress has to depend not only on more generous contributions of money but also on training more persons to do the work.

Paul G. Hoffman, Managing Director of the United Nations Special Fund, reported in October, 1959, that there were sixty member nations and some forty territories associated with the UN that would be classified as less-developed. More than a thousand million people lived in these one hundred countries and territories, with an average per capita income in 1950, according to the best estimates, of something like $110 a year. Mr. Hoffman declared that in the crucial decade of the 1960's, if an explosive situation was to be avoided, it would be essential to raise this average income to at least $160 by 1969. In his opinion, the world might look forward to a general abolition of illiteracy, chronic hunger, and ill health by the year 2000, provided the way is opened for a rapid growth of public and private investment.

EDUCATION, SCIENCE, AND CULTURE

When the DDT team has left the village and the mosquitoes and bugs are, for the time being, dead, then what is going to happen? The people will sleep better of nights, and before long they will notice that fewer people have chills and fever. But will they then join enthusiastically in the march of progress, or will they go on with their ancient customs, merely hoping that some day the spray team may come back and clean up the bugs for them again?

Most people, and especially those who cannot read, are conservative in their ways. They may have heard of the wonders of progress, and may have seen a few of the magic tricks of science. But they do not quickly see how many of their ancestral customs they would have to change if they want to enter the new world where such tricks are done.

It is not even enough to learn to drive a jeep. Someone has to know how to worry about unusual noises in its interior. It is not enough to be rid for a while of the large visible insects that can be killed by DDT. Someone has to learn to worry about dirt and deadly creatures that are invisible. And that is only the beginning. The higher the standard of living rises the more things have to be attended to and the more the people have to know in order to make the system work.

Education, therefore, is a special requirement that has to be supplied with all the other kinds of development in agriculture, health, industry, or political-economic institutions. Not only must the people who will do the work, from vaccinating to banking, be trained for their jobs, the whole population has to be educated to believe in progress and to accept necessary changes without too much delay. This necessity for keeping all parts of the procession com-

31

ing along is a common source of trouble in even the advanced nations. As the less-developed nations hurry to take on the methods of modern science, there will be the same kind of troubles. Parts of the social and political system will be slow to develop the new qualities that are necessary to make the new projects work successfully.

The UN Educational, Scientific, and Cultural Organization, known as UNESCO, grew out of conferences among the governments in exile in London during the last years of World War II. The Nazi invasion of western Europe in 1940 had destroyed a large part of the educational system of the conquered countries. The governments of those countries knew that after liberation their schools and universities would need books and equipment, new buildings, and new teachers to replace those who could not be found. So a Conference of Allied Ministers of Education was formed in London to study reports of damage and to look for means of restoration as soon as their countries should be liberated.

In the meantime the Allies began planning for a United Nations Organization, and it was evident that the new organization would have to take an interest in education all over the world. The London Conference of Allied Ministers began to invite representatives from other countries outside of Europe. The United States sent a delegation to the Conference in April, 1944.

The United States belief in mutual understanding as a means of building friendship and peace has deep roots in tradition. For instance, in 1859 Abraham Lincoln told a farmers' meeting:

> From the first appearance of man upon the earth down to very recent times, the words "stranger" and "enemy" were quite or almost synonymous. . . . Even yet, this has not totally disappeared. The man of the highest moral cultivation, in spite of all which abstract principle can do, likes him whom he does know much better than him whom he does not know. To correct the evils, great and small, which spring from want of sympathy, and from positive enmity among strangers, as nations or as individuals, is one of the highest functions of civilization.*

* Address to Wisconsin State Agricultural Society, Milwaukee, September 30, 1859.

The need for wide international contacts in education, science, and culture was clear to the delegates from all over the world at San Francisco. The UN Charter authorized the UN to promote the formation of an affiliated agency for educational and cultural development. A conference for that purpose met in London in November, 1945, and wrote a constitution for the United Nations Educational, Scientific, and Cultural Organization which was signed on November 16, 1945.

UNESCO exists in its own right by virtue of the fact that its members have accepted its constitution. Its members are not necessarily members of the UN. Its regular revenue does not come from the UN, but from the direct contributions of its member nations. The organization's General Conference, meeting once every two years, adopts its budget and assesses the contributions from the members. The routine management is carried on by an executive board of twenty-four members.

Fundamental Education

Less than half the world's children go to school. In the region of South Asia and the Pacific, for instance, about 55 million children out of a total of 95 million have no schooling whatever. One immediate result of the lack of schools in so much of the world is that most of the human race cannot read or write. Progress cannot go far along modern lines in communities where hardly anyone can read.

But UNESCO has found that where most of the people cannot read, learning their letters is not usually what they need to begin with. They need to learn some simple practical improvements in their way of life that they can quickly understand and accept as good. Perhaps the first thing is to learn to boil the ditch water before drinking it. Perhaps they need the idea of digging a latrine, or of building a raised cooking place instead of using a fire on the ground where cattle and children get mixed with the cooking pots. They can learn to build better houses out of local materials, and usually they can improve their food supply by planting a vegetable garden.

When the people have tried a few simple novelties and have found them acceptable, those among them who have already thought of the advantage of knowing how to read will find it easy to convince the majority. Then if a teacher with the modern visual aids and other equipment can be had, learning to read is easy. By this time the crust of ancient habits and customs may have been cracked. After a while the outsiders can leave for another village, and there is a chance that local people will go on under their own steam, digesting the new methods and ideas into their own culture, so that instead of a foreign development there will be a native growth with live roots in the soil.

For a job of this size, teaching hundreds of millions of people, UNESCO cannot itself find the money to hire enough teachers. What UNESCO can do is to show the various member nations how to go at it, and it can supply certain kinds of training and equipment.

Many countries have peculiar language problems, especially where a country has dozens of separate languages. Often the only way the different tribes can talk together is in a foreign tongue such as English or Spanish. Where the pupils need to learn English for practical use, they do not need to start with Shakespeare. UNESCO specialists can expedite the practical teaching by sorting out the common words that are most useful in daily work and concentrating on those.

Pictures are being used more and more in teaching at all levels of schooling. A team of visual-aid experts ran a three-month seminar in New Delhi, in 1952-53, to teach Indian teachers how to use film strips, pictures, and other visual materials in fundamental education. Another UNESCO team was sent to Sicily to help the government in fundamental education and the use of visual aids.

A more ambitious project is the launching of training centers for teachers in fundamental education work. The first of these was opened in Patzcuaro, Mexico, for Latin American teachers. It graduated its first class of forty-six students in November, 1952. The Arab States Fundamental Education Center was opened the following year in Egypt, in a building erected by the Egyptian Government. The courses include methods of teaching reading and writing, home economics, health, agriculture, and cottage industries. The centers publish books on educational methods as well as readers, primers, and visual aids such as film strips. Working with the United Nations Relief and Works Agency, UNESCO has also directed schools for 125,000 young Arab refugees in the Middle East.

The UN is particularly interested in promoting the spread of free and compulsory schools among the new independent countries of Asia and Africa, and wherever in the world people are just now coming into the duties and problems of self-government. The UN believes that if these new nations are to become successful democracies their people must have all the schooling they can get as quickly as possible.

The value of world-wide technical exchange can be illustrated by the new processes that are beginning to revolutionize the manufacture of books and newspapers. The changes run from new ways of making newsprint paper out of straw, bagasse, and hardwoods, to photographic composition and printing that can be used effectively even with the complicated alphabets of Asia. This new technology appears to point toward cheaper books and newspapers and toward better chances for small, competitive printing enterprises to flourish. The spread of these methods may considerably speed the process of fundamental education.

One of the important requirements in fundamental education is for simple books in all languages on subjects that the students feel the need to know about. If there is no such reading material at hand, many of those who learn to read will quickly forget. Another danger is that most of the books that poor people can get at low prices will be trash material not in line with the civilizing purposes of the UN. It is therefore doubly important for UNESCO to promote the use of printed material telling about the United Nations and the Declaration of Human Rights, to make known to the people the fact that they live in a world that may be friendly to them. UNESCO has begun the promotion of public libraries as pilot plants in India, Colombia, and Nigeria. The project in India is the first public library open to all castes and creeds in that country, and is reported to serve about 2,300 persons daily.

Books, Records, and Films

UNESCO helps to expand international traffic in literary materials, phonograph records, and motion-picture films.

A UNESCO report on the work done in 1952 listed as "probably the most outstanding accomplishment in the cultural field" the signing of the International Copyright Convention, sponsored by UNESCO. This agreement protects the rights of authors and artists in books, plays, music, films, painting, and sculpture, in all the countries ratifying the Convention.

UNESCO has sponsored agreements for temporary importation free of duty of press, photo, radio and other equipment for international reporting, and of films to be viewed by potential users.

The Universal Postal Union, at UNESCO's request, has acted to simplify the handling of books and periodicals between nations. In 1960, UNESCO invited member states to reduce tariffs on the works of living artists.

The shipment of delicate scientific instruments across national boundaries had been inconvenient because when the customs officials looked into the package they often damaged the contents. UNESCO therefore sponsored an international agreement by which customs examination can be done at the laboratory while the instruments are being packed or unpacked by experts who are familiar with how to handle them.

Museums

A well-managed museum will draw many thousands of visitors who, even if they do not spend time there for serious study, will be sure to learn something as they pass through. They learn what things look like in other parts of the world, and how things looked in past ages. They may get a new light on the physical sciences as well as on geography, history, and art.

This kind of education may help to make people willing to have their country cooperate with other countries, and it therefore is worth promotion by UNESCO. Accordingly, UNESCO holds conferences in various parts of the world for museum directors and other specialists to exchange information about how museums can best be used in popular education.

For the Blind

At the suggestion of the government of India, UNESCO undertook in 1949 to promote standardization of Braille, the written alphabet of the blind, as it is applied to various languages throughout the world. Blind students who use more than one language would be benefited by using the same symbols so far as is practicable. Standardized Braille would be especially useful in countries where people commonly speak several languages, and where the language of higher education or of religion is different from the ordinary speech. UNESCO published in 1954 a basic reference book on the use of Braille in various languages by Sir Clutha Mackenzie, one of the ablest leaders of the blind.

As a result of these efforts, by 1957 enough uniformity had been achieved so that a blind person could read his own language even though printed in a foreign country; and in the main the Braille symbols all over the world now represent the same sounds—which is more than can be said for the visible letters of even the common Western alphabet.

A conference of blind musicians was held at UNESCO House in Paris in 1954, to improve the standardization of Braille music notation as it is used in different countries. This conference was attended by musicians from Europe, North America, Latin America, the Middle East, India, and Japan. The conference voted for a permanent organization under the World Braille Council, which had been set up by UNESCO in 1952.

Coupons

In the first years after World War II, UNESCO promoted the supply of books and educational equipment for countries where dollars were scarce, by issuing international coupons to educators in those countries, which could be used for purchases in the United States and other "hard-currency" nations. By 1960 this program had moved material to a total value of over $30,000,000.

The coupon scheme was so successful that another plan was added. Gift coupons are for sale in countries that produce many kinds of educational material—the United States, the United Kingdom, the German Federal Republic, the Netherlands, France, Australia, and Canada. Private persons and organizations in these countries may choose a Project from a UNESCO catalogue of Gift Projects. The donor buys UNESCO coupons and sends them to the Project. The Project can then use the coupons as a kind of money order in the currency of the country from which they came. An additional advantage of this system is that it may help to set up contacts between people in different countries who are interested in education.

Still another coupon scheme provides help for students to travel in foreign countries where they need foreign money for expenses. These coupons are intended mainly for people from soft-currency countries who cannot convert their money into the currency of the countries where they plan to go.

Science and Culture

Many of the specialized agencies of the UN are devoted to scientific progress and the engineering applications of science. Their fields often touch or overlap, and they cooperate at these points in joint activities. UNESCO helps the member nations to expand scientific education and training. In the spreading of cultural materials and international cultural contacts UNESCO is the chief UN agency.

UNESCO enterprises include making a world survey of mathematics textbooks, encouragement of national associations of science teachers, preparation of traveling scientific exhibitions, and publication of articles on scientific research.

In 1959, UNESCO issued inexpensive sets of color slides made from its collections of paintings from Iran, India, ancient Egypt, and Yugoslavia. It sent expert missions to Peru, Syria, Iraq, Israel, Egypt, Colombia, and Yugoslavia to advise on the preservation of ancient monuments, and is aiding the United Arab Republic and the Sudan in a campaign to save the ancient monuments now located where the new Aswan Dam would flood them.

In 1957 UNESCO adopted three major projects, planned to take up a considerable portion of the Organization's efforts and resources over a period of six to ten years. One is the extension of primary education throughout Latin America; another the encouragement of research on the use of desert lands; and the third the promotion of understanding and appreciation between the cultures of the Orient and the Occident. The third project will make use of all channels of education and information, and particularly of travel and study grants.

In the dry-lands program UNESCO has helped to set up research stations to study not only the scientific aspects but also the traditional knowledge and skills of the desert people. The countries with desert lands send delegates to meetings to discuss such questions as dry-land biology, climatology, water supply, and energy sources. This major project is scheduled to be finished in 1962.

The Oceans

The first world congress of ocean scientists was held at UN Headquarters in September, 1959, under the joint sponsorship of UNESCO and the Special Committee for Oceanic Research of the International Council of Scientific Unions. More than a thousand scientists from 45 nations attended the congress.

The scientists discussed the possibilities for extracting vitamins, antibiotics, and hormones from sea plants and animals, and for mining certain minerals, such as manganese, from the sea floor. They talked of plans for drilling through the earth's crust where it is thinnest, under the sea, in order to help answer questions on the age of the earth's crust and the original formations of the seas. From Japan came a proposal for a world-wide study of radioactivity of sea water, in preparation for control of the disposal of radioactive wastes from atomic power plants, which might lead to dangerous poisoning of the oceans.

The fact was pointed out that a congress on ocean science could be most appropriately held under UN auspices, since the more intensive study and use of ocean resources will raise new questions of international law, which will naturally come before the United Nations for consideration.

The UNESCO Constitution provides that each member state shall make arrangements for bringing its educational, scientific, and cultural organizations in touch with UNESCO, preferably by forming a national commission.

In the United States, for example, a National Commission for UNESCO was established by an Act of Congress. About eighty private organizations, ranging from the American Association for the Advancement of Science and the American Farm Bureau Federation, to the Congress of Industrial Organizations, the Negro Newspaper Publishers Association and the U. S. Junior Chamber of Commerce, are affiliated with the National Commission. The one hundred Commission members are appointed by the Secretary of State. The affiliated organizations nominate sixty members; most of the others come from federal, state, and local government. The Commission helps the government in its relations with UNESCO; it helps in recruiting experts for UNESCO missions and suitable delegates for UNESCO conferences. It holds a national conference every other year, and publishes material on UNESCO that it regards as useful for the information of the people of the United States.

The many-sided work of UNESCO represents a part of the many-sided life of the human race. It represents the healthy peacetime interests of people all over the world. It helps to build up the sane side of human life, in the hope that the sane part of the human mind will in time get the better of the part that falls into war. Nevertheless, UNESCO has been criticized by people hostile to the United Nations, especially by some of those in the United States who are known as "isolationists." In order to determine whether there was any substance to such attacks, in 1953 President Eisenhower appointed a committee of three distinguished citizens to study UNESCO activities. The committee reported that UNESCO does not advocate world government or world citizenship in the political sense, does not try to undermine national loyalties, does not interfere with the United States school system, and does not show any evidence of atheism or hostility toward religion.

As U. S. Secretary of State John Foster Dulles said in

transmitting a UNESCO report to the National Commission: "The advancement by UNESCO of human welfare through education, science, and culture promotes international understanding which contributes to peace."

MONEY AND TRADE

International prosperity depends partly on production, partly on the exchange of the money of different countries, and partly on the conditions for exchanging goods and services. The UN has many agencies helping with production, one of which is the International Bank for Reconstruction and Development, which promotes international investment. The International Monetary Fund helps to smooth the exchange of currencies, and the General Agreement on Tariffs and Trade serves as a bargaining market where nations can make agreements to reduce tariffs and other trade barriers.

The World Bank

The International Bank was organized at a conference at Bretton Woods, New Hampshire, U.S.A., in the summer of 1944 along with its sister institution, The Monetary Fund. By 1960 the bank had sixty-eight member nations.

At the start the authorized capital of the Bank was $10 billion. Each member nation subscribed to the stock of the Bank for an amount based in general on its wealth and trade, varying from $3,175,000,000 for the U.S.A. to $400,000,000 for India and $200,000 for Panama. As a rule 2 per cent of the subscription is paid in gold and 18 per cent in the member's national currency. The remaining 80 per cent stands as a guarantee to cover the Bank's liabilities.

Most of the money the bank lends is obtained by selling its bonds in the money markets of the world. In 1959 its volume of business had grown so large that the Board of Directors took action to double the authorized capital, and each member was asked to double its subscription, holding this additional money available for call in case of need. Several members subscribed even more than double, and made considerable cash payments. By April, 1960, the Bank's subscribed capital had risen from $9.5 billion to $18.9 billion.

The Bank can lend to a member government or one of its agencies, or to a private enterprise in a member state if the government guarantees the loan. The Bank is not in business to make money, but it must not be careless with its assets, or they would quickly melt away in a vast sea of desired but unprofitable projects all around the world.

The management of the Bank has five general principles to guide it in deciding whether to lend money in a particular case.

First, it will not use up its funds to finance any operation, however useful, if the borrower can get money from someone else on reasonable terms. This Bank is a public institution set up to increase the total of international lending, not to replace any transactions that will go on without its help.

For instance, since the first job of the Bank was to aid in the reconstruction of war-battered Europe, it started in 1947 by lending dollars to France, the Netherlands, Denmark, and Luxembourg, to be used for buying supplies mainly from North America. When the Marshall Plan came into the picture with a large supply of dollars to be spent for recovery the Bank turned its attention to other fields of action.

The second principle is that the Bank will ordinarily lend a country only the foreign money it needs to pay for foreign supplies and services connected with a project. The Bank has to satisfy itself that the borrower is making proper efforts to raise local capital to pay for the labor and domestic materials that go into the project. For this purpose the Bank often advises on government policies to encourage local savings.

The third principle is that the borrower and guarantor must have a good prospect of paying principal and interest. Not only does the Bank have to keep its capital from being lost, it also has to hold the confidence of investors so that they will buy its bonds.

The project must be an economically sound one in the sense that it will add more to the country's wealth than its cost. If it is a public work that draws an income, like a hydroelectric project, it will usually be able to earn enough direct income to cover its capital investment and interest. If it is a system of free roads, paid for out of tax revenues, it ought to cause an increase in the wealth of the country that would yield the necessary taxes to pay for it. The Bank wants to know that the government is efficiently administrated and that its tax system is adequate to meet the needs of a developing country.

The revenues from an enterprise, whether they are earnings or tax returns, are of course in the money of the country. The main question for the Bank is whether these revenues can be turned into dollars or whatever money is required for payments on the loan. The Bank wants to know whether the government is handling the problems of foreign exchange in such a way that the loan payments can be met along with all the ordinary costs of foreign trade.

The fourth principle is that the Bank will prefer the projects that are most useful and urgent. At best the Bank and all other sources of foreign capital cannot cover everything that growing nations would like to have. The developments include a high proportion of public or semipublic service enterprises—such as electric power plants, roads, railroads, flood control, and irrigation.

Finally, the fifth requirement is that the borrower must have the knowledge, skill, and financial position to carry the enterprise to success. Given a good basic ability to deal with the project, the borrower can get plenty of technical advice and assistance, and the Bank insists that all the necessary experts be called in. The Bank keeps up its interest in the building and operation of the enterprise during the life of the loan.

In the course of its work, the Bank sends missions to member countries, to survey particular projects or to consult on a general development program. In its general development surveys, the Bank cooperates with other agencies that may have an interest in the proposed work, especially the other specialized agencies of the UN.

When the Bank first began to operate in 1946, the great need of all countries was for dollars. The Bank had a nest egg of dollars in the 2 per cent part of the subscriptions, and the United States released its whole

cash subscription of $635,000,000. In 1947 the Bank
sold $250,000,000 worth of dollar bonds in the New
York market. Since that time other currencies have been
in demand, as borrowers found that they could buy machinery and supplies from countries other than the
United States. By September, 1959, the Bank had raised
$2.5 billion in various currencies in addition to its own
capital funds available for loans, which amounted to
about $1.5 billion. At that time the total authorized cap-
ital was increased from $10 billion to $21 billion.

One of the most notable projects using Bank funds is
the Damodar Valley Corporation in India, a development
organization similar to the Tennessee Valley Authority in
the United States. The original purpose of this project
was to prevent the costly floods of the Damodar River.
In 1945 a TVA engineer was called in, and with his
advice the plans were extended to cover a full development of the river, including irrigation, navigation, and
electric power. The Bank made three loans, totaling
$44,500,000 mainly for electric power development in
the Damodar Valley. In addition the Bank has lent
nearly $550,000,000 for railways, ports, aircraft, and
iron and steel production and various power projects in
India.

In recent years the Bank has begun to study the possibilities of atomic power for underdeveloped countries,
especially those where fuel is scarce. Its first loan for
this purpose was made in September, 1959, for a plant in
southern Italy.

Other projects financed by the Bank have included
water power development in Mexico, modern highways in
Ethiopia, a new port in Rangoon, and pulp mills in
Finland.

By October, 1959, the Bank had made a total of 241
loans, amounting to $4.6 billion, some of which, of
course, has already been paid back.

Another kind of work that the Bank has recently
begun to develop is helping to find acceptable settlements
for financial disputes between nations. The Bank worked
out the amount that the United Arab Republic should
pay to the owners of the Suez Canal which it had seized.
It also gave advice to India and Pakistan about a proposed
agreement on sharing the waters of the Indus River.

The International Finance Corporation (IFC)

This agency was established in 1956 with the special purpose of encouraging the growth of private enterprises in the underdeveloped countries. It invests in such enterprises in association with private capital and management, and without requiring a government guarantee against loss. It judges projects on their merits as investments for private capital, and provides supplementary capital where it will.be most useful. It does not undertake management of projects.

IFC has a capital of about $100,000,000, subscribed by fifty-nine member governments. It is closely affiliated with the Bank but is a separate agency with its own treasury.

IFC made its first investment in June, 1957. By April, 1960, it had made twenty-seven investments for a total of $27,000,000, located in twelve countries of Asia, Latin America, the Middle East, and Australia. The industries involved turn out such things as lumber and rubber products, cement and prestressed concrete, cotton textiles, electrical equipment, and automobile parts.

The International Monetary Fund

The International Monetary Fund is a system of cash reserves that the member nations can draw upon to meet temporary deficits in their international trade.

The Articles of Agreement of the Fund were drawn up by the Bretton Woods Conference in 1944, and came into force on December 27, 1945. Nations that join the Bank must first be members of the Fund. Each member is assigned a "quota" in the Fund and is assessed a subscription usually equal to its quota. As a rule the member pays one-quarter of its subscription in gold, unless that would take more than 10 per cent of its official supply of gold and dollars. The rest of the subscription is paid in the member's own money.

When a country buys more from abroad than it can sell abroad, it has to find some kind of foreign money to pay the deficit. Ordinarily such payments are drawn from the country's reserves of gold or of foreign money— generally pounds or dollars. If these reserves start to melt

away with frightening speed, the country will take some
kind of action to reduce its trade deficit.

There are some ways of dealing with a trade deficit that
are harmful to world trade, since they consist of setting
up trade barriers to keep out foreign goods. There are
other remedies that are not harmful to world trade. But
they take longer; they may not be within reach of a country with only a small reserve. The main purpose of the
Fund is to be a supplementary reserve that in favorable
cases will make possible a sound adjustment of the member's international trade position.

The Directors of the Fund have discretionary powers to
restrict or expand the amount of help they will give to a
member, according to whether they think the member is
taking the correct actions to balance its trade. The Fund
cannot encourage a member simply to lean on the Fund
when it has a deficit, without doing anything to cure the
deficit. Such actions would fritter away the Fund's hard
currency without lasting benefit to the members. The
Directors therefore consult regularly with the member
governments about their financial policies and advise them
about possible improvements.

The Fund is particularly interested in bringing about
what is known as "convertibility." The British pound
sterling, for instance, would be convertible if a dealer
coming into the money market with a thousand pounds
could freely change them for dollars, francs, or any other
kind of money he might want. Another ideal is the stabili-
zation of exchange value. The pound is stable if it will
always bring the same number of dollars or ounces of
gold.

If a country has been having trouble keeping its reserves, it may resort to exchange restrictions of some
kind, which limit the amount of that country's money that
anyone can turn into gold or dollars. If the country decides
to make its money convertible, it removes these restrictions. But it looks with apprehension at what may happen
next.

The chief danger, when money is made convertible, is
it may be exposed in time of stress to a heavy demand
for converting the local money into foreign currencies.
This creates a "run on the bank" that might be disastrous.
If such a run develops, the "bank may have to close."

That is, the government puts back the exchange restrictions, and is left in a weaker position than before.

Why, then, should a country want to take the risks of removing exchange restrictions? The removal is an exercise of financial strength to take advantage of the profits of free trade. The country can then shop around freely to buy its imports wherever it can get the best bargains. It will also have to sell abroad in unprotected competition with its rivals. This necessity may scare some of its businessmen, but if they can stand it they will become productive and safer against inflation of their costs.

If all the principal countries can make their money convertible, world trade will be increased and will be more efficient. Goods will be bought and sold in the most profitable markets. The Fund devotes much of its attention to advising nations on how to become financially strong enough to take the risks of convertibility with good prospects of success.

There are two kinds of devices that countries can use for balancing their trade when they are failing to sell enough abroad to balance what they buy. One kind of treatment is designed to make people in the country buy less from abroad; the other kind is designed to get foreigners to buy more of what the country has to sell. The first kind includes tariffs, which raise the prices of foreign goods in the country. It also includes restrictions on imports or in the use of money, which directly cut down the buying of foreign goods. The international trade organizations aim to persuade countries to avoid these devices as far as possible, since they stifle trade.

The second kind of treatment for balancing trade is made up of devices for selling more goods to foreigners. One way is to "devalue" the currency, or reduce its value in ounces of gold. Then a foreigner with gold or its equivalent can buy more of the devalued money than before. This is the same as offering a special discount to foreign buyers, for the internal prices paid by citizens do not change much, if any, when the money is devalued in gold. The United States devalued the dollar in 1933 to promote exports; and the countries of Western Europe devalued their currencies in 1949.

The members of the Fund have agreed not to devalue their money more than 10 per cent without getting the advice of the Fund. Frequent changes in the value of money are disturbing to trade because they make dealers fear to sign contracts for future payments.

The device that is most approved for stimulating exports is to keep prices down—in other words, to avoid inflation. If there is not too much money in circulation in the country, compared with the goods and services for sale, prices will hold down, and foreign buyers will be attracted. On the other hand, if there is too little money, there will be deflation, and prices will fall so far as to cause unemployment. The government's problem is to adopt policies that will lead to the correct balance between inflation and deflation, and the correct balance between encouraging exports and maintaining full employment.

If the government knows how to adopt the right policies, and if the voters will stand the short-term discomforts that go with such policies, a country may be able to balance affairs internally and externally at the same time. Since this condition leads in the long run to the highest combination of prosperity and real income, it is worth some sacrifices if it can be attained. The Monetary Fund advises the members on how to attain the right balance.

The exact measures that are needed to put a country in sound condition vary with circumstances, but in the main they consist of actions that governments can take if they are allowed to do so by the voters.

To prevent inflation there are two principal financial devices. One is to raise taxes and cut public spending until the correct state of budget balance is reached. The other is to raise the government "discount rate," which will cause higher interest rates generally and discourage borrowing. The discount rate is the rate of interest that the commercial banks have to pay if they borrow from the central bank, or, in the United States, from the Federal Reserve banks.

The general principle of budget balance, now well understood by financial experts, is that in depression the government should run a deficit so as to give the people more money to spend. Then if a boom comes on, the government should reverse and run a surplus, so the people will have less money to spend. If the price level is satisfactory as it is, then the budget should have only enough deficit to create the money each year that is needed to carry on the growing volume of business. No one can hit the ideal levels exactly, but governments can come close enough to do fairly well in stabilizing prices.

The reason for raising the discount rate in a threatened inflation is that too many people are borrowing money from the banks to use for investment or spending. If interest rates go up they may put a damper on this borrowing. The effect is not as powerful as the effect of budgetary changes. Many countries leave their official discount rates unchanged for years at a stretch.

Aside from these two financial devices, the principal way to avoid inflation is by speeding the advance of technology. Increased efficiency of production reduces costs and allows prices to come down while real wages go up. This is the most valuable adjustment, but it takes a long time. It serves as underpinning for the sound financial policies that are able to take effect more rapidly.

In the underdeveloped countries, the inflation danger is likely to arise in connection with economic development. New factories can be built with the people's savings, or with foreign money invested in the country, with comparatively little danger. But if the program is pushed too fast it may be financed by government borrowing from the banks, which is in effect the same as printing the money. Too much of this may poison the new development with inflated prices that discourage real savings and chill the whole program. The techniques for holding to a sound development policy call for expert advice which can be obtained from the Bank and the Fund.

How does the Monetary Fund do its work? First of all, it consults with countries that are protecting their trade balance by artificial trade barriers, advising what policies to adopt for improving their fundamental strength. Then it stands ready to help out as the member countries take one step after another toward freer trade.

Each time a country loosens up on the bandage that is restricting its trade, it may start to bleed a little from its gold and dollar reserve. If the loss is soon stanched, the new adjustment is a success. The circulation is improved and the country is stronger. During this process, the country may supplement its own reserve by purchasing the currency it needs from the Fund, paying in its own currency. It may need dollars or pounds or some other money to take care of a temporary deficit while trade is getting adjusted to the new rules.

When a country is past the adjustment period, and has built its reserve to a new safe level, it can restore its position in the Fund by buying back its own currency for dollars, or other freely convertible currencies, or for gold. By March 31, 1960, members of the Fund had repurchased over $2 billion worth of their currencies.

The amounts that members can get from the Fund are limited in various ways. They have almost free rights to draw currency to the amount of their gold deposit, and a limited right to sums in excess of that, with an over-all limit generally equal to their quota. The Directors may allow a country a stand-by account that it can draw upon in case of need. They can stretch these limits for specially useful adjustments that the Fund wants to encourage. The Fund provides money only for adjustments that it is convinced can be carried through in three to five years. It is not in the business of making long-term investments.

For each accommodation the member pays the Fund a service charge of 0.5 per cent. If the amount purchased is larger than the member's gold subscription, he pays an additional charge which starts three months after the transaction at 2 per cent a year and increases with time and with the size of the purchase in relation to the member's quota. These stepped-up charges are intended to put pressure on the member to set his house in order and buy back his currency. The money received is used to defray the Fund's expenses, though that is not its chief purpose.

In the first years after 1945, the Monetary Fund had little to do. The troubles of the member nations were so deep-seated that no temporary help could cure them. For the time, they had to protect themselves with trade barriers until they could build up their production. But as the war damage has been repaired and business has improved, the Fund has had more and more opportunities to promote the free exchange of money that is the lifeblood of healthy world trade.

By April, 1960, the Fund had sixty-eight members, and had sold various currencies equivalent to a total of nearly $3.5 billion.

During 1959 and 1960 most of the members voluntarily increased their subscriptions by 50 to 100 per cent. The total assets of the Fund, which in January. 1959, amounted to $9.2 billion, were increased through these new subscriptions to more than $14 billion.

On the whole the members have continued to keep their policies in line with the Fund's objectives, and each year has brought some degree of progress toward currency convertibility. They have made increasing use of the opportunities for technical cooperation, and have become well accustomed to referring important questions of foreign exchange policy to the Fund for advice.

General Agreement on Tariffs and Trade

In 1945 the Economic and Social Council decided to call a Conference on Trade and Employment, with the hope of reducing tariffs and other trade barriers. A preparatory committee was given the job of drafting a charter for an International Trade Organization, which the proposed Conference might establish.

The Conference met in Havana in 1947 and 1948 and adopted a charter for the ITO, but that organization has so far failed to come into action for lack of acceptances from the member nations, particularly the United States. In the meantime the preparatory committee decided to go ahead with more informal negotiations for tariff reductions. This latter operation soon became a success, and led to the General Agreement on Tariffs and Trade, known as GATT. The United States and all the other principal trading nations joined in the GATT conferences.

In these conferences, each member nation comes in with a list of other people's tariffs that it hopes to get reduced, and a list of its own tariffs that it might reduce in the course of bargaining. The rule is that if any two countries agree to reduce certain tariffs for each other's benefit, they must give everyone else the same reduction. The conferences also take up other kinds of trade barriers, and consider complaints about members that violate their agreements.

The effect of GATT has been a notable reduction in obstacles to trade. Along with the Bank's assistance to the international flow of capital, and the Fund's help in the exchange of money, the general situation of world production and trade since the Bretton Woods Conference has shown an encouraging rate of improvement.

TECHNICAL SERVICES

The modern world depends on many kinds of technical service to make possible the most efficient production and distribution. Some of the necessary services have to be international. Several UN specialized agencies are devoted to providing these international technical services.

It is noteworthy that these technical organizations, which deal only with experts and are generally unknown to the ordinary man in the street, began to appear long before the grass-roots services such as WHO and FAO. Probably the main reason for this difference in timing is that the techniques for directly attacking disease and poverty developed later than those for services such as telegraph and mail. The progress of international action from legalistic and technical abstractions to the provision of human everyday services is one of the main reasons for the increasing vitality of the idea of international cooperation.

International Telecommunication Union (ITU)

ITU is the oldest of the specialized agencies, having been founded as the International Telegraph Union in 1865 in Paris. In 1932 the radio agreements were added. A revised governing Convention went into effect at the beginning of 1954. The central office of ITU is in Geneva, Switzerland.

The principal work of ITU is to persuade the nations to agree to a practical allocation of radio frequency bands. It also tries to establish the lowest practicable rate schedules for radio, telegraph, and telephone services. ITU committees study and report on engineering problems, from radio ground-wave propagation to the design of telegraph apparatus and the protection of telephone lines from corrosion. ITU publishes technical literature and collects and reports on technical papers published by others.

The Administrative Radio Conference of the ITU which met in Geneva in 1959 had two main problems: the establishment of an international frequency list and the preparation of a plan for high-frequency broadcasting. The radio spectrum has to be allocated to many different types of service, such as maritime and aeronautical communications, weather reporting, broadcasting including TV, amateur radio, and various kinds of scientific work including astronomy.

ITU takes part in the Expanded Program of Technical Assistance, sending experts to advise countries that are developing their communications, and granting fellowships for specialists to study abroad. In Ethiopia, for instance, by 1960 more than five hundred telecommunications employees had been trained in fourteen different subjects in an ITU institute.

Universal Postal Union (UPU)

The Universal Postal Union was established in 1875. In that year the Universal Postal Convention, proposed by the Postal Congress of Berne, Switzerland, in 1874, came into force. Meetings of the Postal Congress are held every five years to examine the rules of UPU and keep them up to date. From the beginning the members agreed that for a reasonable charge every member would have the right to send its mail over any other member's transport services, and that mail coming in from abroad would be delivered without extra charge. The members are also pledged to handle foreign mail by the best means of transport used for domestic mail.

The international postal services include not only letter mail but also parcel post, insured mail, money orders and traveler's checks, collection of bills, and subscriptions to newspapers and magazines.

UPU has set up a Consultative Commission on Postal Studies, to collect information on new technical methods such as mechanized sorting, stamp-selling machines, the most efficient organization of post offices, and the use of special rates for jet-plane service. UPU advises the UN in technical assistance on postal questions, and makes arrangements between different countries for "direct technical assistance" by exchange of specialists and information. In 1960, UPU was preparing an international dictionary of postal technical terms in many languages to be published in 1962.

A nation may join UPU if two thirds of the members agree. In 1959 there were 100 members. Headquarters are in Berne.

International Civil Aviation Organization (ICAO)

In 1919 an International Commission for Air Navigation was formed in Paris to set up technical standards, and in 1928 the Pan American Convention on Commercial Aviation was drawn up at Havana. These earlier agreements were superseded by ICAO, which was proposed at an international conference in Chicago in 1944. ICAO came into effect on April 4, 1947, on being ratified by twenty-six states.

The chief purposes of ICAO are to promote safety and technical progress in aviation, and to see to it that the member states are fairly treated in the operation of airlines. Since 1945, ICAO has helped the member nations to coordinate the services required for international air transport—such as weather reports, traffic control, radio beacons, and communications. Ocean weather stations also aid surface craft and provide search and rescue services. ICAO arranges special aids for air navigation over sparsely settled areas or regions of uncertain sovereignty.

ICAO cooperates in UN technical assistance, especially in helping the less-developed countries to set up ground services for civil aviation, pilot training, instruction in aircraft maintenance, and the organizing of airlines and government civil aviation departments.

In 1959, ICAO was mainly concerned in helping the members to supply the enlarged airfields and services required for jet planes, and was beginning a study of the problems of supersonic passenger liners, including the problem of noise. The growth in size is illustrated by the fact that a pair of the big Boeing jet planes of 1959 could carry more passengers across the Atlantic per year than the Queen Elizabeth, and burned more fuel. As an over-all measure of air safety progress, ICAO reported that while deaths per hundred million passenger-miles in 1945 had been 4.9, in 1958 they were only 1.1.

To avoid confusion, ICAO has introduced codes of standards and recommended practices, which are in effect in all member countries. These codes cover such questions as the licensing of pilots; the right of way in the air; traffic controls; safety rules; airworthiness and the simplification of customs, immigration, and inspection regulations at airports.

ICAO deals with the organization to be provided by each member to rescue the victims of aircraft accidents, and the system of inquiry into the causes of accidents. It has proposed international treaties of agreement on various legal questions, such as recognition of property rights in aircraft, and compensation for damage caused by foreign aircraft falling in a country.

The ICAO basic agreement authorizes its elected representatives to arbitrate disputes between the member nations over air rights. Its first such case was between India and Pakistan. India complained that Pakistan refused to let Indian aircraft fly over Pakistan territory from New Delhi to Kabul in Afghanistan. The representatives took up the dispute in 1952. In January, 1953, they approved an agreement that not only allowed Indian planes to pass but provided for Pakistan to ship fuel to Afghanistan so that the planes could refuel in Kabul for the return trip. This settlement was accepted by both governments—a valuable example of cooperation, in view of their unsettled disagreement over Kashmir.

World Meteorological Organization (WMO)

The main purpose of WMO is to help establish a network of weather stations and a quick exchange of weather information. It promotes standardization of weather observations and uniform methods of reporting. It helps to find ways of applying meteorology to aviation, shipping, agriculture, and other activities. Finally, WMO encourages research and training in the science of meteorology.

One of the jobs of WMO is to publish the *International Cloud Atlas,* containing pictures of hundreds of typical clouds in polar, temperate, and tropical skies, together with instructions for observing and classifying clouds and a summary of the present scientific knowledge of cloud formation.

WMO organizes technical assistance to countries that want advice on setting up weather services or on the use of weather services in agriculture, public health, and industry. WMO teams have worked in Afghanistan, Haiti, Israel, Libya, Turkey, and Yugoslavia, for example. WMO fellowships allow students to study weather techniques in countries that have well-developed services.

A special WMO commission is studying the best arrangement of networks of observation stations. In the 1952 −53 season, whaling ships in the south polar seas were brought into the weather observation network for the first time. Another technical project is the development of apparatus for transmitting weather charts by radio. Others deal with the detection of coming thunderstorms, the classification of snow, and an observation manual for the crews of aircraft.

In preparation for the International Geophysical Year (July 1, 1957 to December 31, 1958), WMO laid out the weather observation program and set up standard methods of weather reporting. In 1960 it reported studies of the 13,000,000 weather observations recorded during the Geophysical Year. It also reported research on use of artificial satellites for weather forecasting, and an investigation in British East Africa of the use of weather information in combating locusts.

Control of Narcotics Trade

International traffic in habit-forming drugs is controlled by the producing and importing nations under terms of a series of treaties made between 1912 and 1948. Legal shipments to each receiving country are based on technical estimates of that country's needs for medical and scientific purposes, and the producing countries are under obligation not to export more than the required quotas.

The enforcement of these treaties is supervised by three United Nations organs, the Commission on Narcotic Drugs —successor to a similar committee of the League of Nations—and two specialized agencies, the Permanent Central Opium Board and the Drug Supervisory Body. These agencies handle the estimates and trade statistics that govern the quantities of various drugs that can be legally shipped.

Not all countries are parties to the drug treaties, but since a legal shipment of any dangerous drug must have both an export permit and an import permit, it is hard for any country to avoid the system. There is, of course, some smuggling, and sometimes a country evades the rules. But world public opinion is so strongly set against illicit drug trading that all governments are sensitive to the effects on their international standing if they are accused of cheating in their relations with the UN system of supervision.

Intergovernmental Marine Consultative Organization (IMCO)

IMCO was established on January 3, 1959, to promote the highest standards of navigation and safety at sea. Among its first activities was the proposal of two international agreements, one on safety and one on prevention of pollution of the sea by oil. Other interests of the organization are the promotion of uniformity in measurement of ship tonnage, and simplifying of the voluminous paper work required for ships entering or leaving port. Headquarters of IMCO are in London.

Economic Commission for Asia and the Far East (ECAFE)

ECAFE is one of three regional commissions attached to the UN Economic and Social Council. This is the first organization in history that has brought together most of the nations of the Orient to discuss their problems and plans. Its main task is to help in developing the production and trade of the area extending from Pakistan to Japan, including the islands of the Western Pacific.

In connection with industrial development, for instance, ECAFE has studied the general conditions for effective foreign aid programs, has recommended the development of national income and resource budgets, and has suggested principles for planning how to bring in new industries without upsetting the standard of living.

ECAFE has made surveys and supplied information about developments in the steel industry, electric power, mineral resources, small-scale industries, housing, and building materials. It has given special attention to the problems of financing economic growth, the promotion of trade, and the design of flood control and water resource conservation. It has cooperated with FAO in a study of the economics of agriculture and in promoting land reform. ECAFE helps in the organization of training centers and study tours. In 1949, it organized a conference in Singapore on inland transport, out of which grew the Inland Water Transport Tour, mentioned in Chapter 1.

ECAFE's Bureau of Flood Control and Water Resources Development has organized a project for surveying the resources of the Mekong River, one of the greatest rivers of the world, which runs out of the mountains of Tibet through the countries of Laos, Thailand, Cambodia, and the Republic of Vietnam. The four governments were enabled in 1958 to begin work on a five-year, nine-million-dollar investigation, with contributions from the United States, New Zealand, France, and the UN Technical Assistance Board.

Headquarters of ECAFE are in Bangkok, Thailand.

Economic Commission for Latin America (ECLA)

This commission is composed of representatives of all the nations that have territories in the Western Hemisphere —the American countries and France, Holland, and the United Kingdom. ECLA has headquarters at Santiago, Chile, and a branch office in Mexico City. It deals with the planning and management of economic development.

The Commission has discussed how to make more capital available in the Latin American countries, both by attracting more foreign investment and by encouraging local savings. It has recommended that the Latin American nations expand trade among themselves, especially by improving transport facilities. It has made studies of agricultural credit, forestry, mineral resources, and trade problems, including balance of payments. The Commission studies how to expand the trade of Latin America with Europe and the United States. It has asked member governments to consider encouraging the immigration of European workers as well as migration within Latin America.

Other subjects that the Commission has worked upon include rural health, tourism, supplies for educational institutions, and arrangements for cooperation with the Inter-American Economic and Social Council. ECLA studies of trade in Latin America have stimulated the Central American nations to undertake the organization of a common market free of trade barriers among themselves, and similar studies are under way for the rest of Latin America.

Economic Commission for Europe (ECE)

In 1946 the most urgent problem in Europe was to revive production and trade, so that people could eat and could repair the devastation of war. The United Nations Economic and Social Council, which was established in that year, examined the situation in Europe and suggested a regional organization to coordinate reconstruction work. The Assembly in December, 1946, directed the Council to establish an Economic Commission for Europe.

All the European states that belong to the UN are members of ECE, together with the United States. European states that do not belong to the UN are allowed to attend ECE meetings and to take part in committee work. The Commission meets once a year; most of the ECE work is done by special committees. The staff is part of the UN Secretariat.

One of the most valuable features of ECE is that of all the regional organizations in Europe it alone, being directly under UN administration, has members from both Eastern and Western Europe.

ECE committees carry on a vast amount of technical work that is necessary for the smooth running of trade and industry in Europe. They arrange for the return of railroad cars, allocate scarce coal supplies, and promote standardization of spare parts. The ECE Committee on Agriculture studies and reports on such matters as farming methods for small farmers, tenancy regulations, and cooperative credit. The Committee on Electric Power makes technical studies and helps to untangle the legal problems of hydroelectric projects on boundary rivers. Other committees deal with the engineering industry, housing, steel, timber, inland transport, and the development of trade.

The staff of ECE issues an annual *Economic Survey of Europe* and a quarterly *Economic Bulletin for Europe,* which are authoritative guides for many kinds of economic planning by European governments.

Economic Commission for Africa (ECA)

ECA was established in 1958 to aid in coordinating the economic and social development of the African nations and territories. In addition to the rapid emergence of independent states in Africa, economic and social progress there has also been impressive since World War II.

Governments in Africa are taking an active interest in promoting the growth of agriculture and industry. Countries that have depended mainly on subsistence farming, together with organized production of a few export crops or minerals, are turning to modern diversified economic activity, with all its problems as well as its advantages. These developments are the particular field of interest for ECA.

Headquarters of ECA are in Addis Ababa.

All these technical service agencies and commissions deal with the organization of the modern economic system. Many of them are unknown to the ordinary man in the street or the man on the farm, but what they are doing makes the difference between primitive ways of living and the full use of science and invention.

The technical services are more closely related to the behavior of governments than they are to the everyday thinking of the people. These commissions and conferences bring together the experts from all over the world to discuss hard scientific facts. They decide what needs to be done in order that industry and trade can be carried on efficiently. Then they report to their home governments, putting them under pressure to cooperate in a great network of practical relationships.

The network of cooperative technical services may not be enough to guarantee peace and good will on earth. But working together for constructive purposes can create a tendency toward friendly feelings among governments as well as among peoples.

HUMAN RIGHTS

According to the Charter one of the main purposes of the United Nations was "to reaffirm faith in fundamental human rights." In Article 56, also, the Charter lays an obligation on the member states to cooperate with the Organization in promoting universal respect for human rights and freedoms and universal observance of them.

The Charter does not describe in detail what it means by these rights and freedoms. The details were left to be worked out by the Organization.

Defining right and wrong so as to gain the acceptance of eighty-odd different nations is not simple. People of different races and religions in different parts of the world do not agree on some questions—such as, for instance, the rights of women. Moreover, there are differences in the meaning of the word "right"—between the right to a fair trial, for example, and the right to good public health services or to a fair chance to find a job. The different moral aspects of these classes of right have been clearly recognized in the UN debates.

Another point has been clearly recognized. No nation on earth can truly say that it gives its citizens absolute legal justice, on one hand, or absolute protection against poverty and ignorance on the other. But the delegates believed that setting up the best ideals that the majority would agree to would help the world to make progress toward those ideals. Even if the nations could not boast of perfection, they could continue to reaffirm their faith in human rights.

The Universal Declaration of Human Rights

To lay down the general principles of right and wrong the Assembly authorized the Economic and Social Council to appoint a Commission on Human Rights. The Commission was directed to draft a Declaration of Human Rights for adoption by the Assembly. Then in order to bind the nations to give serious attention to these principles, there was to be a Covenant, guaranteeing certain rights of the citizen. Any nation that would ratify the Covenant would be "taking the pledge" to abstain from certain forms of injustice and oppression against its own people.

The Commission was appointed in 1946 and spent several years in discussing how to put into words the great principles of the Declaration. It received advice from many other UN agencies and from outside organizations interested in various aspects of right and wrong.

In general it can be said that all rights that need to be upheld are the opposites of wrongs that someone is suffering. A bill of rights therefore starts with a bill of wrongs that need to be corrected. When the United States Constitution was being adopted some of the states refused to ratify it until they were assured that a Bill of Rights would be added. They wanted a guarantee that the new government would not oppress their people with the same wrongs that had led the colonists to revolt against the British Crown. Thus the United States Constitution forbids the government's forcing the citizens to give house room to soldiers in peacetime, because the British Army had been brutal in this respect in its treatment of colonial families. In the same way the UN Commission studied the common wrongs of the twentieth century in all parts of the world, including ancient, almost prehistoric, horrors revived by Hitler and other totalitarian rulers.

All the wrongs of modern times that were a source of trouble or fear anywhere in the world were raw material for the Commission on Human Rights. The Rights of Man, now as in any previous age, are the right not to suffer the common wrongs of the time.

The Universal Declaration of Human Rights was finally adopted by the Assembly without a dissenting vote on December 10, 1948. The Declaration proclaims the universal right of all persons to life, liberty, and security of person; to freedom from arbitrary arrest; to freedom of movement and residence, of speech, press, assembly and worship; and to the other legal rights commonly protected by democratic constitutions.

The Declaration also proclaims the rights of people to

social security, education, and opportunities to earn a living. These rights are recognized as being in a different class from the legal rights usually described in a constitution. The United Nations makes the distinction between "civil and political" rights on the one hand, and what it called "economic, social, and cultural" rights on the other. In general, the civil and political rights, if they are stated in the constitution of a country, can be enforced by law. A man who is arbitrarily arrested and held without trial, for instance, can appeal to a court for a fair trial according to law. If the courts are so corrupt or so tainted with dictatorship that the citizen cannot get his constitutional rights, his nation is guilty not only of oppressing the people but also of violating its own laws.

With the economic, social, and cultural rights the situation is different. No country so far has discovered how to give its people full employment under good working conditions all the time. No country knows how to treat its people with moral justice beyond all criticism, nor how to give the people all the education and health that can be desired.

But governments can do much to help in promoting health, education, justice, and prosperity. The weight of world opinion, in fact, stands behind those in any country who would blame the government for unsatisfactory conditions. For example, the Economic and Social Council at its 1950 session decided to discuss the problems of full employment once every year. Governments, it declared, would achieve and maintain full employment in an expanding world economy under conditions ensuring fundamental political and economic freedoms to the individual.

In any country, a person who suffers a legal wrong and who can get no redress from the courts is the victim of tyranny or misgovernment. If the democratic voting processes are working fairly well he and others of like mind may hope to defeat the government in an election and bring in a government that will properly enforce the laws. Or, if the wrongs go so deep that free elections are impossible, those who are wronged will look for opportunities to overthrow the government by violence.

A citizen who is hurt by unemployment or by bad health conditions or other circumstances may blame his government for neglect of its duty. In this class of dispute, the citizen cannot appeal to the courts; for his complaint is only that the government has failed to pass the right laws to help in correcting unemployment or high rates of disease. In democratic countries such forms of discontent ordinarily serve as ammunition for the opposition political parties. If the discontent is sufficient it leads to a change of government at the next election.

Whether the citizen's appeal is to the law or to the political decision in the next election, or, in a dictatorship, to the processes of resistance, in all cases the moral support of the United Nations acts to encourage the citizen in hatred of injustice. Even the most tyrannous governments do not tell their people that the government glories in doing wrong. The arguments are over what is right and what is wrong. When the secret police drag a man away at midnight and send him off to a concentration camp, the government explains that it is protecting the nation against treason. When a dictator holds an election in which the citizens are not allowed a free choice, he does not boast of the wrong, but proclaims his election as the free and democratic choice of the people. But when the Assembly of the United Nations gives its judgment, that judgment has a thundering authority as the voice of mankind. Arbitrary arrest without due process of law is clearly defined and clearly condemned. An election will not be recognized as free and democratic if it is done under oppressive conditions.

The Universal Declaration of Human Rights, therefore, can properly deal with both the duty of nations to treat their people justly, and the duty of nations to serve their people as well as possible in the promotion of health, prosperity, and social security. The Declaration is not a law, but a statement of moral judgment. It is a set of principles to which a nation can appeal in complaining against another nation before the General Assembly. It is also a set of moral standards to which private citizens or political parties can appeal in complaining against the behavior of their own government.

The Covenants

In the Declaration, the Assembly addressed the nations and told them its judgment on the nature of right and wrong. Beyond that, the Assembly directed the Commission on Human Rights to draft a Covenant to be placed before the nations in the form of a treaty to be ratified.

After some discussion the Commission recommended the submission of two Covenants, one covering legal and political rights, and the other economic, social, and cultural rights, since these two kinds of rights are different in their relation to laws and constitutions. This suggestion of dividing the substance of the Declaration into two separate Covenants was accepted by the sixth session of the Assembly in 1951.

A nation ratifying the first Covenant would bind itself to make and enforce laws protecting its own people against unjust and cruel treatment. There is, of course, no enforcement power in the UN to force a nation to keep such a promise—except the power to receive complaints and to proclaim that wrong is being done. Any nation does not lightly put itself in a position to be openly convicted of wrongdoing.

A nation ratifying the second Covenant would acknowledge its duty and responsibility to do all it can to promote better living conditions. In connection with this general duty, it would also recognize certain legal rights connected with economic and social security. The right to join trade unions, for instance, comes in the second Covenant as a necessary economic right to promote the public welfare.

Many democratic countries have constitutional guarantees of some rights that are not included in the UN Covenants. These are rights of historical or local importance that a majority of the delegates did not regard as necessary in a world statement of principles. The Covenants therefore have to provide that ratification will not reduce any rights already established in a ratifying country.

In 1960, the Assembly was still considering the Covenants without arriving at a final form, for many differing cultural and economic traditions, social philosophies, and legal systems must be reconciled before the rights named in the Covenants can be defined and organized into documents that will be internationally acceptable.

In addition to working on the Covenants, the UN is promoting the principles of human rights in various other ways. The 1950 session of the General Assembly, for instance, proclaimed December 10 as Human Rights Day.

This anniversary is celebrated in many countries with ceremonies to remind the people of the Declaration and to spread the knowledge of its principles. The UN actions on a number of special problems also serve to illustrate and buttress the general principles of the Declaration.

Freedom of the News

One of the most complex rights is that of freedom to give and receive the news. A UN conference on this subject, held in the spring of 1948 in Geneva, adopted three draft conventions: one on gathering and sending of news, one on the right of governments to demand correction of news that they claim to be false, and one on freedom of information.

The first of these proposals would ask the nations to agree that foreign newsmen could have the same right to get at the sources of news as the native newsgatherers. The second convention, on the right of correction, would bind all governments agreeing to it that whenever a news source in any country gives out any item that is objectionable to another member of the agreement, the offended country can send an official complaint to the government of the country where the story originated. Then the government receiving the complaint promises to give it due publicity. Ten governments had signed this convention by the middle of 1960.

The third convention deals with freedom of information, a subject complicated by the fact that it includes on one side the freedom of newsmen and publishers to get and give out the news; on another side the freedom of the people to read or hear the news; and on a third side the rights of governments to protect themselves. The right of publication is easily corrupted into the publication of false reports. The rights of government are easily corrupted into censorship and the "big lie" techniques of public deception. The simple purpose of UN action might be to protect the public's right to full and honest news; but there are some governments that are not ready to grant the public any such right without reservations. The result is that the moral authority of the UN in this matter is less certain in its pronouncements than in dealing with other rights.

Genocide

Genocide is the subject of a special convention adopted on December 9, 1948, by the General Assembly and submitted to the members for ratification. The ratifying states agree that the crime of genocide consists of trying to destroy a "national, ethnical, racial, or religious group as such." Genocidal actions include killing members of a group because they are members, causing them serious injury in body or mind, or trying to destroy the group by preventing births among its members or by transferring its children to other groups. The ratifying states agree to the punishment of any of their citizens who commit genocide, including public officials responsible for genocidal policies.

Of course, a state seriously determined to practice genocide might not hesitate to deny all the facts, whether it had signed the convention or not. But the convention helps to bring to a focus the force of world opinion which even dictators are not entirely able to disregard. As of 1960, sixty-three states had acceded to or ratified the Genocide Convention.

Rights of Women

The Economic and Social Council established a Commission on the Status of Women in June, 1946. This Commission deals with the political and legal rights of women, and such matters as equal opportunity in education and employment.

The Assembly adopted a Convention on the Political Rights of Women on December 20, 1952, and submitted it to the member nations for their ratification. Any nation joining in this convention admits the right of women to vote, to hold public office, and to serve on public institutions, such as juries, without discrimination. In some countries the laws do not grant these rights to women and would have to be changed before the government could become a party to the convention. By 1960, forty-two countries had signed this convention. Another, to protect women against automatically losing their nationality if they marry foreigners, came into force in 1958, and by April, 1960, had been signed by twenty-five states.

The Commission receives yearly reports on the status of women in the dependent territories and has recommended that UN missions sent to inspect conditions in these territories include women members as well as men, so as to promote equal rights of women there.

The Commission has made detailed studies of marriage laws and customs in different countries, and in 1960 adopted a draft of a convention designed to prevent various ancient practices, such as polygamy, marriage of children, or marriage without the consent of both parties, and to secure the registration of marriages. Other subjects of study include a number of inequalities in the position of women in various countries, which will not be easily or quickly changed. One of these is the difference in opportunity for employment in the public service. Another is unequal pay for women doing equal work with men. Another is the unequal position between men and women in the holding of family property and in other legal features of the family relationship. Still another is the unequal opportunity in most countries for women to get an education. All these will require long discussion which in itself will create pressures toward more equal treatment of women in many countries.

Rights of the Child

The Declaration of Geneva, adopted September 26, 1924, by the League of Nations, set forth the rights of the child, and served as the inspiration for a similar action by the United Nations. In 1946 the Social Commission and the Commission on Human Rights were given the responsibility of drafting a new Declaration, which was unanimously adopted by the General Assembly on November 20, 1959.

The Declaration of the Rights of the Child proclaims that every child on earth should have special protection and opportunity to develop in a healthy and normal manner in conditions of freedom and dignity, to have a name and a nationality, and to have proper food, shelter, recreation, and medical attention. He should be given special care if he is handicapped, or in time of disaster; he should be protected from cruelty and exploitation and from any form of discrimination. Finally, the child shall be brought up "in a spirit of understanding, tolerance, friendship among peoples, peace, and universal brotherhood."

Prevention of Discrimination

The Commission on Human Rights has a Subcommission on the Prevention of Discrimination and Protection of Minorities, which has made a series of world-wide studies on various kinds of wrongs done to minorities. A report on discrimination in education, presented in 1957, was taken over for follow-up by UNESCO. The second, on discrimination in employment, was taken up by ILO. A report on religious discrimination and oppression was discussed in January, 1960.

This report stated that oppression on account of religion had been dying out, but that new outbursts of racial and religious hostility in various parts of the world were ominous, and the trend toward religious tolerance might be reversed. The report proposed a set of rules that should be recommended for the guidance of the nations, to prevent oppression in regard to the right to keep or change religion, and to show religion or belief, particularly by different forms of worship; pilgrimages; methods of disposal of the dead; religious holidays; dietary practices; marriage rites; religious training; the taking of an oath; conscientious objection to military service; and secrecy of information given in confidence to a cleric.

Other forms of discrimination studied by the Subcommission have included the denial of political rights and of the right of a citizen to leave any country, including his own, and return freely to his own country. These recommendations were approved by the Economic and Social Council.

War Victims

Prisoners of war and refugees have presented a heartbreaking situation since the beginning of World War II.

Millions of men, women, and children disappeared without trace in the course of the war. Some of them are alive, and those who are lucky may still find trace of their surviving relatives. Most of the missing persons are dead, but there are no records of their deaths. One of the results of these disappearances is to tangle the legal titles to property. The heirs cannot get a clear title. Another is that the wife or husband of a missing person may not be permitted to remarry without positive proof of death.

The Economic and Social Council brought up the subject of the missing-persons problem in 1948. As a result the Assembly called a special conference of governments at UN Headquarters in March, 1950, which set up a Convention on the Declaration of Death of Missing Persons. The Convention provides for a bureau that will examine such evidence as may be obtainable. When it finds no reason to the contrary it will declare a missing person dead, for purposes of fixing the legal position of his survivors.

Under Hitler some of the prisoners in concentration camps were used for "scientific experiments" which left them alive but crippled in one way or another. The plight of the surviving victims was considered by the Economic and Social Council and was brought to the attention of the Secretary-General of the UN. The Secretary-General did not question his own right to inquire on behalf of the UN, although Germany was under occupation and was not a member of the UN. He inquired of the Allied High Commission in Germany, the Federal Government (West Germany), the German Democratic Republic (East Germany), and various international agencies interested in helpless persons.

As a result of these inquiries, the German Federal Government accepted responsibility for the care of the several hundrd unfortunates who could be located. The Economic and Social Council notified the authorities in other countries and various public and private agencies that were in a position to help in locating victims not living in West Germany.

Prisoners of war continued to be a cause of dispute after 1945 because so many of them failed to return.

In 1950, the Assembly received a memorandum from Australia, the United Kingdom, and the United States on the fact that many prisoners of war captured from Germany and Japan had not returned to their homes. The three governments noted that all the victorious Allies had agreed among themselves to repatriate the war prisoners, and they accused the Soviet Union of failing to do so. They asked the Assembly to seek out the truth of the matter and try to secure the release of the survivors.

The Assembly requested the Secretary-General to set up an impartial commission for the examination of these charges. It urged all the governments concerned to co-operate with the commission.

The U.S.S.R. objected to having the subject considered, on the ground that when the UN was founded it was not given any right to deal with the settlement of the war. The Soviet delegation also denied that the Soviet Union was holding any prisoners.

The Secretary-General announced the commission in June, 1951. It was made up of Countess Bernadotte, whose husband had been murdered when he was acting as mediator for the UN in Palestine; Judge José Gustavo Guerrero, Vice-President of the International Court of Justice; and Judge Aung Khine, Judge of the High Court, Rangoon, Burma. Such a committee was well calculated to represent the untrammeled conscience of mankind and to serve as a dependable guide to world opinion.

In 1957 the commission reported that because of the refusal of the Soviet Government to cooperate it had not been able to negotiate directly with that country, but that some progress had been made by direct negotiations between countries and by the good offices of the Red Cross. More than 28,000 Germans had been repatriated, mostly from the Soviet Union, and more than 33,000 Japanese, mostly from China. Some progress had been made in getting names of prisoners who had died. The West German Government, however, stated that it had the names of 87,000 prisoners of war and 16,000 civilians who had been taken by the Soviets but whose fate was unknown.

Refugees

Another large-scale problem left over from World War II was that of the refugees. The International Refugee Organization, which was formed by a number of governments to take care of the war refugees, was dissolved in 1949, leaving the remaining part of the burden to be taken up by the United Nations. The Office of the United Nations High Commissioner for Refugees began operations on January 1, 1951.

The High Commissioner's office was made responsible for the interests of most of the people in the world who have fled from their home countries and dare not go back for fear of persecution. Exceptions are refugees who have been given national rights in the country where they now are, and some others such as Palestinian Arabs who have a special agency looking after them. In 1960 there were still more than a million surviving refugees coming under the High Commissioner's mandate.

The UN pays only for the expense of running the Office of the High Commissioner and its various branches, a total of less than a million dollars a year. The expense of taking care of the refugees is paid for from voluntary contributions, public and private.

The High Commissioner is responsible for the international protection of refugees, the promotion of activities that will help the refugees to find secure homes, and the coordination of private organizations that work for refugees. International protection is necessary because the laws of most countries have no place for foreigners without passports or other evidence that they belong somewhere. A "stateless" person may be refused the right to enter a country at all.

Accordingly, the refugee problem has stimulated international action to define the legal position of people without a country. A Convention Relating to the Status of Refugees was adopted in 1951 at a Conference of Plenipotentiaries held in Geneva. By 1960 it had been signed by seventy states. This convention is designed to make clear what people are refugees and what rights they shall have. Other international agreements provide for the settlement of refugees in the countries where they are living, and for giving refugees the benefit of social security and medical assistance. The High Commissioner has the authority under a General Assembly resolution to make agreements with governments to improve the condition of refugees.

In December, 1958, the General Assembly proclaimed a World Refugee year from June, 1959, to June, 1960, to focus the attention of the nations and people of the world on the still unsettled thousands of refugees in various countries. The following November, Dr. Auguste R. Lindt, the High Commissioner, reported encouraging progress, though by no means a complete disappearance of the problem.

In Europe, for instance, the number of unsettled refugees had been reduced since the autumn of 1958 from 160,-000 to 110,000 despite the influx of 6,000 new ones during the year. The Hungarian refugees in Austria had been reduced from 15,000 to 10,000. In other parts of the world, there were still serious refugee problems; in Tunisia and Morocco, where some 18,000 people from Algeria live in scattered huts, and in Hong Kong there were still some thousands of European escapees from Communist China, together with about one million Chinese.

By February, 1960, the High Commissioner's special program for handicapped refugees had begun to show results. Canada, for example, had accepted 279 refugees belonging to families including tubercular patients, and Sweden had taken more than 3,000 who would be rejected by less generous countries.

Race Conflicts in South Africa

In the first session of the Assembly, in 1946, India complained about the treatment of Indians in the Union of South Africa. One of India's chief accusations was that the Land Tenure and Representation Act of 1946 forced the segregation of Indians both for living quarters and for business.

India said the situation was likely to cause unfriendly feelings between the two countries, and that it violated a treaty and the UN Charter. South Africa replied that segregation was a domestic question which the UN had no right to meddle with, and that the agreement quoted by India was not a treaty. South Africa also pointed out that the UN Charter mentioned human rights but did not say what they were, and that until there was a UN bill of rights, telling just what rights were included, the UN could not find anyone in violation of the Charter on that score.

The Assembly rejected a South African proposal to ask the International Court of Justice whether this matter was purely domestic. Instead, the Assembly said that friendly relations between two member states were plainly being impaired. It advised South Africa to conform with the previous agreement and with the Charter.

In its seventh session, in 1952, the Assembly found the dispute no nearer to a settlement. Meanwhile thirteen Asian states, ranging from Lebanon to the Philippines, brought in a complaint against the South African policy known as *apartheid,* for segregating the Negroes. The Assembly set up a three-man commission to study the race situation in South Africa. It also passed a resolution declaring that where several races live together in a country they ought to be equal before the law. The Assembly affirmed that racial discrimination was contrary to the pledges of the members who had signed the Charter, and solemnly called on all members to conform to their Charter obligations. South Africa refused to accept these resolutions.

In the eleventh session of the General Assembly India and Pakistan again complained of the treatment by South Africa of people of Indian origin. The question was discussed in January, 1957, without the South African delegation, which had been withdrawn from the Assembly in protest against the decision to discuss it. A resolution was passed urging South Africa to negotiate.

In 1959 the Assembly still found South Africa refusing to change its policies. On apartheid, a resolution expressing disapproval and deep concern was passed by a vote of 62 to 3, with 7 abstaining. The delegates that did not vote for the resolution declared that their governments were opposed to race segregation, but that they regarded apartheid as a domestic policy of South Africa, in which the UN had no authority to interfere. But the vast majority of the nations recognize that oppression in any part of the world is a blot on civilization and in the long run a danger to peace, and therefore a matter of concern to the nations assembled in the UN. Moreover, the troubles in South Africa are becoming more dangerous as more and more new independent nations, governed by the native peoples, are established on that continent.

South Africa has, of course, the legal power to defy the opinion of the United Nations, since no one will start a war to force South Africa to change its laws. But the moral pressure goes on increasing with the passage of time. South Africans who support their government's white-supremacy laws cannot escape the knowledge that the world regards their country with disapproval and distaste.

The fact that the power of the General Assembly is moral rather than legislative or military has made it increasingly hard for wrongdoing nations to persuade the Assembly that it has no legal right to discuss any and all moral questions and to pass judgment on what the member governments do to their own people. This development tends to make hard the way of the transgressor, and apparently it will continue to do so.

The Hungarian Question

On October 28, 1956, the Security Council met and took up the question of the Hungarian revolt, in spite of Soviet objections. Three days later Imre Nagy, Hungarian Premier, cabled the United Nations saying that Hungary had withdrawn from the Warsaw Treaty by which she was allied with the Soviets, and asking the Assembly to discuss the matter. He also said that Soviet armies were invading the country. But within the next few days Nagy was overthrown and the Kádár government, supported by the Soviets, took over. In the Council a resolution calling on the Soviets to end their interference was vetoed by the Soviet delegate, and the question then went to the Assembly, which passed a similar resolution on November 4.

For two months the Assembly tried to send observers to Hungary, but they were refused admittance, and at last on January 8 it set up a special committee consisting of representatives of Australia, Ceylon, Denmark, Tunisia, and Uruguay, to find out the truth and report.

The Soviet and Kádár position was that the revolt had been a minority uprising of reactionary elements stirred up and aided by "outside imperialists," and that the Hungarian Government had asked for Soviet help. They denied the stories that trainloads of Hungarians had been carried off to the Soviet Union. They said that the affair was a domestic Hungarian matter which the UN under its Charter had no right to discuss. The special committee was refused permission to set foot in Hungary.

The committee heard 111 witnesses who had escaped from Hungary, including government officials, managers of state enterprises, journalists, professors, lawyers, engineers, and labor leaders, as well as leaders among the "freedom fighters," students, railroad workers, and nurses. One witness had been a manager in the uranium mines, and another a stenographer for the secret police. The committee also examined a mass of documents, including reports from embassies in Budapest. It regarded the testimony as conclusive, and so did the Assembly. The committee's report, submitted on June 20, was accepted by the Assembly on September 13 by a vote of 60 to 10, with 10 abstaining. Only the Communist countries voted "No."

The resolution passed by the Assembly noted the committee's conclusion that the events in Hungary "constituted a spontaneous national uprising," and went on to state flatly that the Soviet Union, "in violation of the United Nations Charter, has deprived Hungary of its liberty . . . and the Hungarian people of the exercise of their fundamental human rights." The resolution stated that the Soviets had imposed the Kádár government on the Hungarian people, had carried out mass deportations, and had violated treaty obligations; and it called upon them to restore the rights of Hungarians and return those who had been deported. It appointed Prince Wan Waithayakon of Thailand as a special representative to bring pressure on the Soviets, and decided to keep the question of Hungary on its program for further discussion.

What good did all this do the Hungarians? Very little, at the time. But it is necessary to keep in mind that no power on earth could drive the Soviets out of Hungary by force, except by starting World War III. What can be done, however, is to deny false stories, tell the truth, and condemn acts of violence and oppression, in a voice that must be heard and respected. No nation that is trying to influence the people of the world to follow its lead and take its side can shrug off the loss of confidence that a UN condemnation inflicts upon it in the eyes of the world.

That is what could be done, and the UN did it. In the long run such an action is a setback for tyranny and a gain for freedom, even though the run may be long. What more could any human influence do, if we are not to blow up the world?

Reports coming from Hungary in 1957 indicated that after the Assembly demanded an end to mass deportations many who had been deported were brought back and further deportations were "substantially diminished."

Slavery

In 1947, the American Federation of Labor asked the United Nations to make a complete study of forced labor in all member states and to take action to get rid of it. (The A.F. of L. had collected a large mass of testimony from released prisoners and escapees describing conditions in the Soviet Union and its associated states, which it wished to bring to public attention.)

The Economic and Social Council received the A. F. of L. request and invited the International Labor Organization and the Secretary-General to study the problem. In 1951, the Council adopted a proposal, put forward by Britain and the United States, to set up a committee of inquiry. The committee was told to study "systems of forced or corrective labor which are employed as a means of political coercion or punishment for holding or expressing political views."

The Secretary-General and the Director-General of ILO appointed Sir Ramaswami Mudaliar, who had headed the Indian Delegation at San Francisco in 1945; Mr. Paal Berg, former Chief Justice of the Supreme Court of Norway; and Sr. Felix Fulgencio Palavicini, formerly Mexican Ambassador to Britain.

The committee sent a questionnaire to all states whether members of UN, of ILO, or of neither. It also invited all private organizations with information on forced labor to come in and testify. Most of the countries of the world replied to the committee's questionnaire, and a number of organizations and private persons gave evidence. The committee decided to send out to all the interested governments a summary of the testimony. It reported to the Assembly that the Soviet Union and the states associated with it employed forced labor on an extensive scale.

In September, 1956, a UN conference in Geneva

adopted an antislavery agreement, bringing up to date a League of Nations agreement of 1926. The new treaty goes beyond the well-known kinds of slavery to forbid such things as debt bondage, serfdom, bride price, inheritance of wives, and certain abuses in the adoption of children. The agreement had been signed by thirty-nine states as of April, 1960.

It is worth noting that the practice of employing convicts in a prison factory or on highway construction, as is done in many civilized countries, was not the target of the "forced labor" investigation, which applied only to the punishment of *political* prisoners. Merciful treatment of criminals is also important as a matter of human rights, but is not in the same classification with the problem of political slave-camps.

The duty of governments to protect their people from epidemic diseases, economic depressions, and widespread ignorance, can no longer be denied. But this duty has only recently been recognized and governments are slow to shake off old ways and take on new responsibilities. The United Nations helps to push the nations along the way they must go to find better conditions of life for their people.

The moral pressure of the United Nations—pressure on reluctant nations to give up legal wrongs—is a striking example of the power of united action. The advance of justice and mercy can often be pushed with the greatest effect by the moral pressure of people not injured themselves but shocked by cruelty to others. Wrongdoers are extremely sensitive to condemnation by the "public"—that is, by the people whose disapproval may be injurious to their success. This sensitivity of nations is constantly proved in the meetings of the UN Assembly and the Security Council. No nation boasts of wrongdoing; if a nation is determined to do evil it looks for ways to evade the judgment of the world.

When an overwhelming majority of the Assembly, made up of delegates of many races, religions, and languages, passes judgment, there is no more formidable judgment to be had on earth.

NON-SELF-GOVERNING PEOPLES

The age of modern European imperialism began with the opening of sea routes from Europe to Asia around the Cape of Good Hope and to America across the Atlantic. After A.D. 1500 most of the world came under European control. Then came a movement for independence, starting in the eighteenth century with the successful revolt of thirteen British colonies on the North American coast, and continuing with the Spanish colonies in Central and South America. The movement for independence, called "self-determination" by Woodrow Wilson at Versailles in 1919, has now progressed so far that the United Nations Assembly treats it as a matter of course. Of about 800 million people who lived in dependent areas in 1945 over 600 million had gained full independence by 1960. Most of them are in India, Pakistan, Indonesia, Burma, the Phillippines, Israel, Morocco, Tunisia, Ghana, Malaya, Cameroun, Togoland, Guinea, Somalia, and Nigeria. The Assembly expects the remaining inhabitants of dependent territories to be trained for self-government and released from control as soon as they are ready to look after themselves.

In the UN there are two systems under which the nations that govern dependent territories give an accounting of how they treat their subject peoples. One is known as Trusteeship, under which the governing nations report to the UN Trusteeship Council. In the other, less formal system, the nations report to the Secretary-General on the economic, social, and educational conditions in their areas.

Trusteeship

The trusteeship system has come down from the mandate system of the League of Nations. After World War I, the former German colonies were taken over by the League. Their administration was farmed out to various powers which accepted a "mandate" to govern in the interest of the people and to give account of their stewardship to the League. These areas became "trust territories" under the United Nations by agreement with the various powers that accepted responsibility for administering them.

In July, 1959, there were ten UN trust territories, all originally League of Nations mandates except Somaliland, which was taken from Italy in World War II. They were: in East Africa—Ruanda-Urundi, administered by Belgium; Somaliland, administered by Italy; and Tanganyika, administered by the United Kingdom. In West Africa— the Cameroons, administered by France; the Cameroons administered by the United Kingdom; and Togoland, administered by France. In the Pacific area—Nauru, administered by Australia, on behalf of Australia, New Zealand and the United Kingdom; New Guinea, administered by Australia; Western Samoa, administered by New Zealand; and the Trust Territory of the Pacific Islands, administered by the United States.

The UN Charter established a Trusteeship Council to look after the interests of the people in the trust territories. On the Council are all the UN members that hold trusteeships and an equal number of other members.

The Council sends out a questionnaire of several hundred detailed questions on the political, economic, social, and educational progress of the trust territories. It also receives hundreds of petitions and complaints from organizations and individual people in the territories.

The Council sends regular missions to visit every trust territory once every few years. The missions are chosen from a wide variety of nations to get a broad view of the problems. For instance, one mission to West Africa had representatives of Iraq, Belgium, Mexico, and the United States. The missions look over the territory, talk with the people, and are ready to hear comments and complaints.

The trustee government is required to submit a full report every year. It sends a special representative prepared to answer questions about the territory. On the basis of all the various sources of information, the Council makes a report on each trust territory to the General Assembly.

The General Assembly in turn discusses the trusteeship reports and makes recommendations for the government of the territories. It does not hesitate to criticize what has been done and to call for more education, better laws, and more signs of progress toward self-government.

Togoland

The Trusteeship Council and the Assembly take a keen interest in old customs that may have been long established in a territory but which offend the moral sense of outsiders. The British Administration in Togoland on the West Coast of Africa, for instance, was asked not only to provide more schools and medical services, but also to abolish corporal punishment. The Administration proudly reported in 1953 that during the previous year a well-equipped hospital was established in the territory, free primary schools were opened, and a new secondary school and two teacher training colleges were established; and finally during the year no court in the territory had sentenced anyone to be whipped. The Council urged the Administration to continue its efforts for the complete removal of corporal punishment from the territorial law.

In 1954 the General Assembly again discussed the Togoland problems at length. Britain called attention to the fact that it was administering British Togoland in conjunction with the adjoining Gold Coast territory. As the Gold Coast was soon to be granted independence, the British wished to drop the Togoland trusteeship.

Representatives from the area indicated a wide divergence of opinion. Some wanted to unite British Togoland with the new independent Gold Coast; others wanted union with French Togoland.

Finally, in 1956, the people of British Togoland were invited to vote on whether to join the Gold Coast in setting up the new state of Ghana, or to continue under British administration pending some other solution of their problems. The voting was orderly and the people voted 93,000 to 67,000 to join the Gold Coast. Accordingly, the territory is now a part of the state of Ghana, which was admitted in 1957 to the United Nations as the eighty-first member.

As for French Togoland, a special UN Commission reported to the Trusteeship Council in September, 1957, that the relations between France and the territory had been much improved by a new governing statute, passed by the French Parliament in the middle of 1956 and endorsed by the votes of over 70 per cent of the Togoland people in October of that year. The new statute gave wide powers to the Togoland Government, reserving to the French authorities only the administrative jobs considered to be "financially and technically onerous." The Commission regarded these jobs as likely to be transferred gradually as local people were trained to take over the more difficult kinds of work. The Trusteeship Council commended the French administration and sent the report along to the Assembly "in order to set in motion the influences that would help to bring further progress toward self-government."

In April, 1958, elections for a new legislature were held under UN supervision. More than 400,000 people voted. After this election the French and Togolese governments agreed that the country would become independent on April 27, 1960, and the General Assembly voting in November, 1958, unanimously endorsed the plan for independence.

The French Cameroons, another trust territory in Africa, also chose independence through a vote of its elected legislature in October, 1958, with the consent of the French authority, to become effective January 1, 1960. The General Assembly, after examining the report of a visiting mission on conditions in the territory, voted to end the trusteeship on that date and recommended that the new nation should be admitted to UN membership on becoming independent.

In the British Cameroons, on the other hand, there was much doubt as to what the people wanted. The territory was administered with Nigeria, which was scheduled for independence in October, 1960. As the sentiments in the northern and southern parts of the country were evidently not alike, the Assembly provided first for a vote in the northern section, on whether to join Nigeria or to put off the decision until some later date. The people voted in

November, 1959, and chose to postpone the decision, by a vote of 113,859 to 70,546, with only 525 votes thrown out as invalid.

The vote in the southern section, however, was deferred because the Assembly became convinced that the issues had not yet become clear enough to obtain a useful decision.

These situations illustrate how the UN purpose of extending self-government to dependent peoples can be peacefully carried out wherever the governing powers are willing and are ready to agree that the people are capable of standing on their own feet.

Somalia

Another good example of how the UN promotes independence is Somalia, formerly Somaliland, an independent nation since July, 1960. This Italian colony was taken by the British in the last war, and its future was left to the decision of the United Nations. The Assembly decided in 1949 that the Somalis were not ready for independence but might be after ten years of development. Italy was appointed as Trustee, with a special Advisory Council of representatives from Egypt, Colombia, and the Phillippines to aid it in its administration. The British turned over the government to the new administration on April 1, 1950.

The Somalis had a hard road to travel before they could expect to stand on their own feet as an independent nation. A population of 1,200,000, made up chiefly of nomadic shepherds roaming over a largely arid territory, they would need to find ways of increasing their earning power, especially in foreign trade. In order for many of them to settle down they would need to tap the groundwater with an extensive system of wells.

They also would have to learn to read and write, not merely in Italian but also in their own tongue. That presented a problem, for there was no written Somali language and the spoken language was divided into many dialects. Two language experts from UNESCO were called to advise the Administration on what form of Somali to make official, and to invent an alphabet in which to write it.

Politically, there were already some definite signs of life. For example, there was the Somali Youth League, strongly anti-Italian, which had been founded in 1943. The Youth League representative told the Trusteeship Council in 1953 that the Administration was moving too slowly. He demanded an over-all economic plan and a native legislature with the right to legislate.

Another representative advised the Council not to be too much in a hurry for political democracy. He said:

> The tribes cannot be disbanded and a new system substituted in a few years. They must be guided and interested by means of appropriate measures so that a gradual transformation takes place until final social, economic, and political progress has penetrated and extended to the entire Territory, creating new living conditions. Somaliland's evolution will be the result of two concurrent movements: first, the development of the parties and of the various administrative and political organizations which the Administering Authority is establishing, particularly in the cities and other centers; secondly, the evolution of the tribes as a result of a diffusion of new ideas and above all of changes in the economic situation.

Despite all the obstacles, the Somalis made good progress in their ten-year training period. The Assembly had decided that Somalia would become independent by December 2, 1960. But the Administration and the new Somali government reported that the country would be ready by July 1, and the Assembly voted to end the trusteeship on that date.

Samoa

In November, 1946, Western Samoa was being shifted from a League of Nations mandate to a United Nations trusteeship, under New Zealand as administering power. The Administrator invited the inhabitants to express their opinions on the proposed trusteeship agreement that New Zealand had submitted to the UN.

The Samoans petitioned for immediate self-government

under the protection of New Zealand. At the suggestion of New Zealand, the Trusteeship Council decided to send a mission to Western Samoa. The mission was made up of members from Belgium, Chile, and the United States. It was in Samoa in July and August, 1947, and at the same time the New Zealand government consulted with the Samoans. In November, New Zealand adopted a new form of government for Western Samoa which was closely in line with the mission's recommendations.

Under the new Samoan Amendment Act, the principal chiefs were established with the High Commissioner in a Council of State. Samoan members had a majority in the Legislature, with authority to make the laws and to dispose of the revenues of the territory. The Trusteeship Council expressed satisfaction with the New Zealand policies and recommended that the Samoans should take on more and more of the responsibilities of self-government.

In 1959 again the Trusteeship Council sent a mission to Western Samoa, and on hearing its report endorsed the New Zealand plan for political development of the territory leading to independence in 1961.

The right of the UN to send missions to look over the trust territories is new. This right did not exist under the League of Nations mandate system. The trusteeship system is considerably broader in its scope and gives the administration of these territories a much more extensive supervision than under the League.

Non-Self-Governing Territories

The trustee areas, containing some 20 million people, represent the direct responsibility of the UN, being in each case the ex-colonies of defeated Powers whose sovereign claims were wiped out by war. As of June, 1960, some 53 other territories, containing 83 million people, are ranked as non-self-governing, and the UN Charter lays an obligation on the Powers that control them to report on their progress each year. Many of these territories have a considerable range of freedom in local affairs, although their foreign relations are decided by the metropolitan power. Others are governed by administrations in which the inhabitants have little or no part.

Information on the progress of non-self-governing territories is sent to the Secretary-General of the UN, who submits it to a special committee for study. It then goes to the Assembly for action. In the Charter the governing countries agreed to send information on only social, educational, and economic conditions in their territories. But the Assembly has repeatedly asked them to report also on the development of self-governing institutions.

In cases where a nation stops sending information the Assembly calls for an explanation of what change has justified erasing the name of a territory from the non-self-governing list. An example was when the United States ratified the Constitution of Puerto Rico, which gave that country the right to choose all its public officials and make its own laws. The United States then classified Puerto Rico as "self-governing" and ceased to report on it to the UN. The Assembly voted to accept the claim that Puerto Rico is self-governing, with the Latin American countries voting "Aye." Similarly, U. S. reports on Alaska and Hawaii were dropped when they became states of the Union.

The Assembly has passed resolutions advising the governing nations to apply the principles of the Declaration of Human Rights to the people of dependent areas, and to take advantage of technical assistance opportunities for developing those areas. Reports on such action are requested. The Assembly has also made clear its insistent desire for progress toward self-government.

Libya

The United Nations, representing the world community, is the natural sponsor for any new nation asking to be born. Korea and Somalia are not the only UN godchildren. Another former Italian colony, Libya, was judged to be politically ready for early independence although it would need technical and economic help in getting established. In November, 1949, the Assembly appointed a commissioner, Adrian Pelt of the Netherlands, as head of an international council to help the Libyans set up a government. The Council met on April 25, 1950, and by December 2 of the same year a Libyan National Assembly had been organized and had chosen the Emir of Cyrenaica as king. A provisional federal government was established in March, 1951, and on December 24 King Idris I proclaimed Libya's independence. The UN General Assembly welcomed the new nation, but it was not admitted to the UN because of a Soviet veto until the "package deal" of 1955.

Foreign help to Libya came from various sources. Financial help has come from Britain, France, Italy, and Turkey. Technical assistance was given in a cooperative program of the United Nations and the United States Point Four. The country started as one of the poorest in the world, but not without hope of improvement. The average income was the equivalent of about $35 per person per year. Eighty-five per cent of the people were unable to read or write, and three hundred infants out of every thousand died before they were a year old. There were no resources except a generally poor soil, a scanty supply of water, and a population largely untrained but with ability to learn and an ambition to improve their way of living.

Most of the work therefore started with education and training. UNESCO gave technical help in starting new schools, and expecially in the training of teachers. Students took training in all sorts of needed skills, from typing and bookkeeping to Arabic and English, geography, carpentry, and mechanical drawing. In the oases of the Fezzan a UNESCO expert from Austria organized education centers to teach the people reading and the use of better tools and better methods of hygiene. A team of olive pruners from Tunisia traveled throughout the country showing how to prune the olive trees so as to get better crops. Sheep were improved by importing better breeding stock from Turkey.

By 1956 Libya was reported to have one of the fastest-growing school systems in the world. Developments in these early years included a successful community center for women in the Fezzan, improvements in vegetable growing as a result of demonstration gardens, and establishment of many literacy centers that soon grew into community clubs. There was also a rapid spread of football and volleyball in the country.

Meanwhile WHO set up a program of public health, and the Libyan Government made a contract with UNICEF to test and vaccinate the children against tuberculosis. An expert from the World Meteorological Organization organized a system of weather reports, important not only for flying but also for modern agriculture. Foreign experts in government have helped the new Libyan administration to set up its necessary public services with a modern budget and tax system and sound foreign trade and banking policies.

In 1959 the World Bank, at the Libyan government's request, sent a mission to Libya to survey the economic situation and help work out a development program. In 1960, the UN Special Fund agreed to contribute $1,000,-000 over a five-year period for an Institute of Higher Technology in Tripoli, to which Libya itself would contribute $2,000,000. The Institute will offer four-year courses in civil, mechanical, and electrical engineering and in food processing.

One might get the impression that there is not much room for Libyan independence. But in fact, every foreign expert came to Libya because the government invited his organization to send him. The Libyans have been working hard to push back the desert and build themselves a prosperous country, using all the expert advice they could get.

South-West Africa

This former German colony was mandated to South Africa by the League of Nations after World War I. It became a serious problem in 1946, when South Africa refused to transfer it to a trusteeship under the UN like the other mandated territories. South Africa took the position that with the death of the League of Nations, the mandate ceased to exist, and that the administering power was no longer responsible to any outside authority. The United Nations has never accepted this position.

In 1949 the General Assembly asked the International Court to give a ruling on the South-West Africa question. In 1950 the Court ruled that South Africa still has international obligations in connection with the territory, according to the Covenant of the League of Nations and the terms of its mandate, and that the right to supervise the administration of the territory now rests in the United Nations, to which reports and petitions should be submitted. The Court declared that South Africa has no right to govern South-West Africa if acting alone but only if acting with the consent of the United Nations.

South Africa refused to accept this judgment of the Court, but it was not absolutely opposed to discussions with the UN about some arrangement for reporting progress, so long as it did not have to submit to any control. In November, 1953, the Assembly set up a Committee on South-West Africa, to act "until such time as an agreement is reached between the United Nations and the Union of South Africa." The Committee was instructed to get what information it could about conditions in South-West Africa and report. The South African Government refused to cooperate with the committee in any way.

By 1959, the South African delegation at the UN was at least taking part in the discussions of South-West Africa, but the report of the Committee was not encouraging. The Committee said it was "particularly disturbed" by the spread of racial segregation and the plans for mass removal of the native peoples from their ancestral lands to make room for European settlement.

During the debate over the Committee's findings, a number of petitioners were heard, despite the strong opposition of the South African delegation. The burden of the testimony was that the native people were suffering desperately low living standards and working under conditions of "near slavery." The government was imposing segregation, cruel punishments, and a system of migratory labor by which families and the traditional social order had been broken up. The petitioners charged that South Africa was planning to annex the country.

A member of the South African parliament spoke on the economic problems of the territory and the efforts that his country was making to build highways and railroads, and to provide dams and wells to help out the meager water supply. He also started that there were 35,000 non-European pupils in schools, as compared with only 2,430 in 1922. The South African Foreign Minister took part in the debate, describing his country's policy, which remained one of firm refusal to make any formal agreement granting the United Nations the right to supervise the administration of South-West Africa. But he gave assurances that "the door will be left open" for further discussions.

The Assembly adopted a series of resolutions criticizing various aspects of the administration of the territory, leaving South Africa once more exposed to the general disapproval of the world.

Self-Determination

Underlying the trusteeship system, the Charter provision for reports on all dependent areas, and the evident enthusiasm for helping new nations to be born and to prosper, is the principle of self-determination of peoples. This principle is not as simple as it looks at first sight.

At Versailles, after World War I, President Wilson tried to stand firmly for self-determination as the Peace Conference worked at redrawing the boundary lines of Europe. At some points he was frustrated by the demands of the victorious Allies who wanted territory for defense purposes or for other reasons not including the wishes of the inhabitants. At other points the principle of self-determination ran up against the fact that hostile peoples lived in the same territory. Some cruel mass migrations have been forced on the peoples of Europe to rearrange them into areas where they could be free of hostile foreigners. And still there are pockets of people who cannot govern themselves because they do not occupy the right land to make a workable nation.

Some of the difficulties in applying the principles of self-determination are illustrated by the experiences of the United States. Until the present century the United States was an expanding power, taking, buying, or conquering the western lands until it came to the Pacific, and at the same time taking in millions of people from other countries, chiefly from Europe and Africa.

Then in the Spanish War of 1898 the United States captured Cuba, Puerto Rico, and the Philippines, and the reaction against imperialism set in. The people of the United States found that they did not want to govern foreign-speaking people in distant lands. They took measures to make these countries independent as soon as the inhabitants could successfully carry out the duties of independent nations.

On the other hand, the United States has made it clear that no state in the Union can resign and set up for itself. This was settled in 1861–65 by one of the fiercest wars in history. The United States recognizes many Indian tribes as "nations" with treaty rights that include a considerable degree of self-government, subject, however, to veto by the United States Congress. But it does not allow immigrant groups to set up independent governments on its soil. They can vote in elections, and can vote as a German bloc or an Irish bloc if their leaders can hold the people together. But they cannot escape the sovereignty of the United States.

These experiences have left the people of the United States strongly in favor of self-determination—but only where it is a practical way of living. They believe that any race or language group that wants to be an independent nation ought to be allowed to do so, provided it can make a workable nation. Being a workable nation means coming to paying its own expenses, helping its neighbors to keep the peace, and cooperating with the United Nations. By these standards not every small group of people that wants self-determination can get full national independence. But world opinion, as shown in the UN, is plainly favorable to the independence of peoples wherever it is practicable.

INTERNATIONAL DISPUTES

One of the most important jobs of the United Nations is to settle international disputes if possible, or if they cannot be settled, to keep them under negotiation without shooting while time passes and passions may perhaps cool. Often the negotiations drag along for years with no final settlement. But as one UN delegate remarked, "It is better that old men get ulcers than that young men get shot."

The United Nations has dealt more or less successfully with many international disputes, great and small. In 1954, a United States Senate Committee report listed twenty-one "disputes or situations" that had been brought before the Security Council up to that time and seventeen "political controversies" before the General Assembly. The following cases are among those that have attracted the most attention.

Syria-Lebanon

One of the earliest cases to come before the Security Council was the dispute over the failure of French and British troops to withdraw from Syria and Lebanon after the end of World War II. In February, 1946, Syria and Lebanon complained to the Council. The cause of the failure to withdraw was not any deep conflict between these countries and the British and French, but a failure of the British and French to agree between themselves on the conditions of evacuation. At the time there was danger that the dispute might be widely interpreted as the beginning of an unfortunate quarrel between two Western Powers over the exploitation of two weak countries of the Near East.

In the Security Council a resolution was proposed "expressing confidence" that the British and French would move out as soon as was practicable. This resolution was blocked by a Soviet veto, but its moral effect was not lessened by that. The British and French evacuated Syria in about two months and Lebanon a few months later.

The Corfu Channel Dispute

In October, 1946, British warships in the Corfu Channel, off the coast of Albania, ran into a minefield and suffered damage and some loss of life. The following January the United Kingdom brought the matter before the Security Council, charging that Albania had laid the minefield and had failed to notify shipping. Albania denied the charge and said that the British had been trespassing in Albanian waters.

A proposal was introduced declaring that Albania was to blame for the minefield, and this motion was vetoed by the U.S.S.R. The United Kingdom then proposed that the Council should advise Britain and Albania to take the question to the International Court. This was passed.

The United Kingdom appealed to the Court on May 22, 1947. Albania agreed to appear, but pleaded that the question was not admissible under the Charter and the Statute on which the Court was established. The Court refused to throw out the question, and held that Albania by agreeing to appear had accepted the Court's jurisdiction.

The two contestants then agreed to ask the Court: first, whether Albania was responsible under international law for the damage and loss of life and whether it should pay compensation; and second, whether the Royal Navy had violated the sovereignty of Albania by its actions in the Corfu Channel.

The Court decided that Albania was responsible for the explosions. It appointed two experts to assess the damages, and on December 15, 1949, fixed the compensation at £843,947 to be paid by Albania to the United Kingdom.

The Court also decided that on the occasion when the explosions occurred, the British had not been trespassing in Albanian waters. But it ruled that in the following month the British had violated Albanian waters, and that the declaration of the Court's judgment was all the compensation for that violation warranted in the circumstances.

Kashmir

When the British Government granted independence to India in 1947, it could not persuade the Hindus and Mohammedans to agree on setting up a single over-all government. After much discussion the new nations of India and Pakistan were formed; one to contain a majority of Hindus and the other a majority of Moslems. A large and cruel exchange of populations took place and there was severe rioting. Blood was hot.

By a part of the agreement the British rulers set free the mountain princedom of Jammu and Kashmir, with the right to decide for itself whether to join India or Pakistan. Shortly afterward there were reports of an invasion by Pakistani tribesmen. India complained to the Security Council on January 1, 1948. The situation was complicated by the fact that most of the population was Moslem, but the Prince, or Maharajah, was Hindu. The Maharajah had decided to join the state to India, and India had accepted.

India complained that Pakistan was guilty of aggression. Pakistan told the Security Council that it had tried without success to control the wild tribes on the border, and that the Maharajah's joining of India was illegal. Both sides were willing to let the people vote on the question once order had been restored.

Th Security Council appointed a commission to investigate and mediate between the contending states.

The Council itself recommended that the two states should call home their people who were not regular residents of the territory, and that they should agree on a cease-fire. As soon as the disorders had quieted down, the Indian army should be reduced to the minimum needed for keeping order. Then there should be a free and impartial election to decide which nation would get the territory. The Council directed the commission to go to India and Pakistan and help to work out an agreement.

When the commission got to India in July, 1948, it learned that regular Pakistani troops were in Kashmir "to prevent a forcible seizure of the country by India." The situation looked more and more like war. The commission therefore proposed to both governments that they agree on a cease-fire and withdrawal of troops. It offered suggestions on how the voting was to be carried out. By December, India and Pakistan had agreed to a cease-fire as of January 1, 1949, with truce details to be decided later. The cease-fire line was settled the following July 27.

The commission then attacked the problem of getting the two sides to withdraw their forces so that peaceful conditions for voting could be established. It was unable to bring the parties to an agreement. In December, 1949, the commission reported a stalemate to the Council, and suggested that perhaps a single UN representative with broad powers might have better success.

General McNaughton of Canada, who was President of the Council in December, made an unsuccessful effort to bring about an agreement. In April the Council appointed Sir Owen Dixon of Australia as UN Representative, and his appointment was accepted by both India and Pakistan.

Sir Owen made a new effort to get a withdrawal of forces, but without success. He reported back to the Security Council and asked to be relieved.

The Council on April 30, 1951, appointed Dr. Frank Graham of the United States as UN Representative, and called upon the two Governments to cooperate with him.

Dr. Graham talked with the Governments of India and Pakistan during the summer of 1951. He found them willing to agree on proposals to avoid open warfare and warlike talk, and on the acceptance of the principle of deciding the issue by a vote. But they could not agree about how and when to demilitarize.

Dr. Graham reported the situation to the Council, which directed him to continue his efforts. The Soviet delegate objected, saying that the UN efforts had been really intended to support a British and American plot to get a military base in Kashmir. He suggested leaving the whole matter to the people of Kashmir.

From then on, as the years passed, both sides reduced their armed forces in the territory, but no agreement on a vote of the people was reached. In February, 1957, the Security Council sent Gunnar Jarring of Sweden to see if any settlement could be agreed upon. He found the leaders of both countries ready to talk with "complete frankness and cordiality," but with no signs of agreeing. India's position was that Pakistan must take all its troops out before India would further reduce its forces in Kashmir. Pakistan said it had brought home its troops but that India was refusing to do its part. Pakistan suggested arbitration to decide whether it had removed the troops or not. India refused on the ground that to submit to arbitration would amount to letting Pakistan have a voice in Kashmir affairs, which would be a violation of sovereignty since Kashmir was already a part of India. Pakistan complained to the Security Council that India was already incorporating Kashmir in the Northern Zonal Council of India, to tighten its ties with India, and gave notice that it would seek further action by the Council.

Mr. Jarring reported that he had no proposals for a settlement but that both India and Pakistan seemed to want to find a solution.

The UN position all along has been that the two parties should hasten to reduce their armed forces in Kashmir and make arrangements for a vote. This UN request has made slow headway. But in the meantime, the shooting was stopped; India and Pakistan continued to sit side by side in specialized agency committees and other UN activities, often voting together. By 1954 the two Governments had established direct conferences between their Prime Ministers, and the danger of war appeared to be over. From 1957 to 1960 the Security Council had no discussion of this conflict, though it received a number of communications from the Governments involved.

Indonesia

Two days after the surrender of the Japanese forces in Indonesia, which had formerly been under Netherlands control, Indonesian nationalists set up a Republic of Indonesia and declared their independence. After serious disorders, political negotiations between the Dutch and the Indonesians finally broke down when the Netherlands launched what it called police action and what the Republic of Indonesia insisted was a military attack. The Security Council succeeded in arranging a cease-fire in August, 1947, and both sides accepted a good-offices committee of Australia, Belgium, and the United States to conduct negotiations for a truce. The Netherlands and the Republic signed an agreement in January, 1948, including eighteen principles to serve as basis for final settlement.

Later the agreement broke down, and there was more fighting. The Council called for a new cease-fire in January, 1949, and recommended that the Netherlands recognize the independence of Indonesia. A conference was held at The Hague later that year, with representatives of the Netherlands, the Republic of Indonesia, other parts of Indonesia not included in the Republic, and the UN Commission for Indonesia. With constant encouragement from the UN, the transfer of sovereignty was finally accomplished on December 27, 1949. Less than a year later, at the next session of the General Assembly, Indonesia was admitted as the sixtieth member of the UN.

Greece

At the end of World War II Greece was left in a badly devastated condition. The Communist states of Albania, Yugoslavia, and Bulgaria lay along the mountainous northern border, in a favorable position to help Communist guerrillas attempting to capture the country. The Greek Army had been shattered, and was too weak to cope with the guerrillas alone. By request of the Greek Government British troops were in Greece to help in its defense.

In January, 1946, the U.S.S.R. complained to the Security Council that British troops were interfering in Greek internal affairs. Greece denied the interference. The Council refused to act and considered the matter closed. Another complaint of Greek attacks on the Albanian border was also rejected. Then Greece asked the Council to look into the aid being given by Albania, Bulgaria, and Yugoslavia to the guerrillas. The three Communist states denied that they were giving any such aid. The Council appointed a Commission to examine the situation on the spot. The majority of the commission reported that the three northern states were helping the guerrillas; the minority, consisting of the Soviet and Polish members, denied it.

In March, 1947, the British were financially unable to go on helping Greece, and the United States took over the job, explaining its action to the Security Council. The United States Congress, in appropriating money for aid to Greece, stipulated that the action should be stopped if

at any time the UN should decide that it was no longer
necessary. The United States would not veto any such
decision. This action strengthened the position of the UN
in the Greek situation.

The Assembly took up the Greek question again in the
fall of 1947, and recommended that Greece and her three
neighbors settle their disputes by diplomacy. It appointed
a special committee, which later reported that Greece
had consented to cooperate but the other three countries
had refused on the ground that it was a violation of their
sovereignty. From that time on for several years, each
Assembly renewed its condemnation of the Communist
aid to the guerrillas and continued its committee to watch
developments.

In time the situation changed. Yugoslavia ceased to give
aid to the guerrillas in Greece. The Greek Army was built
up to such strength that it was able to restore order.
Economic aid helped to rebuild the country, and with
returning prosperity the internal appeal of communism
faded.

In the end, the problem that could not be solved was
that of the return of some twenty-five thousand Greek
children who had been taken north of the border in 1948.
The Assembly asked for the return of children who wanted
to be sent back or who had relatives in Greece ready to
receive them. Yugoslavia cooperated, but other East
European states, where most of the children were believed
to be held, refused to release them.

The Berlin Blockade

In September, 1948, France, the United Kingdom, and
the United States complained to the Security Council that
the Soviet Union had cut off land communications between the Western zones of Germany and Berlin. The Council voted to discuss the blockade as a threat to the peace
—over the protest of the U.S.S.R., which contended that
the measures had been necessitated by currency reforms
in the Western zones that threatened the Soviet zone with
economic collapse. Various members of the Council tried
to find a solution that both sides would accept, but the
proposed draft was vetoed by the Soviets. The President
of the Assembly and the Secretary-General, basing themselves on an Assembly appeal to the Great Powers to

"compose their differences and establish a lasting peace," also urged the parties to hunt for a means of agreement, but with no immediate result.

In the meantime, the Western Powers supplied Berlin by air, with spectacular success, and informal talks among the UN representatives of the four occupying Powers soon led to an agreement. It was universally recognized in this case that a reasonable solution of the trouble would have been much harder to arrange if the opposing parties had not been able to meet easily and informally in the corridors of the UN building.

Palestine

The United Nations inherited the situation in Palestine. That territory had been placed under a British mandate by the League of Nations. In 1947 the British Government asked the UN Assembly to look into the Palestine question. The Assembly held a special session in April and May, 1947, and appointed a committee to recommend what should be done. The committee majority recommended that Palestine should be divided into an Arab state, a Jewish state, and a special area including Jerusalem under an international government. This plan was accepted by the Assembly on November 29, 1947.

The plan provided that the British mandate should end by August 1, 1948, and the new states were to come into existence within two months after the British forces had evacuated the country. It soon became clear that there was going to be trouble between the Jews and the Arabs. The Assembly on May 20 appointed Count Folke Bernadotte, President of the Swedish Red Cross, as Mediator.

The British gave up their mandate on May 15, and the new state of Israel was proclaimed. Soon the Arab states were marching against Israel. The Council called on all governments to abstain from war in Palestine. It issued a cease-fire order on May 22. By June 9 the Mediator had received the agreement of all parties to a truce, starting June 11, to last four weeks.

At the end of the four weeks the Arab states refused to extend the truce, and fighting broke out again. On September 17, 1948, Count Folke Bernadotte and the chief of the French observers, Colonel André Sérot, were assassinated in the Jewish sector of Jerusalem. Dr. Ralph

Bunche, of the United States, who was acting as assistant to the Mediator, was directed to take over.

During the last three months of 1948 there were several outbreaks of fighting, but the truce was restored on January 7, 1949, with troop withdrawal and supervision by UN observers. During the next six months all the Arab states signed armistice agreements with Israel. The Security Council urged the states to negotiate a final peace settlement. Dr. Bunche was awarded the Nobel Peace Prize for his work in Palestine.

The Assembly, on December 9, 1949, directed the Trusteeship Council to administer the international City of Jerusalem, but both Arabs and Jews refused to give up their parts of the city. The Jews even moved in some departments of their government.

After 1949 the relations between Jews and Arabs failed to improve. The UN Truce Supervision Organization reported many violations and disputes. A particularly dangerous dispute arose over the refusal of Egypt to let ships bound for Israel pass through the Suez Canal. Repeated efforts of the Security Council failed to persuade Egypt to lift these restrictions, and the situation remained tense. All the Arab states made it plain that they would never reconcile themselves to the existence of Israel.

Suez

In the summer of 1956 Egypt received large shipments of arms from Czechoslovakia which were stacked in the Sinai Desert, near to the Israeli border. Israel accused Egypt of planning war, and also complained of increasing raids by Egyptian bands known as *fedayeen*. The United States withdrew a previous offer of a loan to Egypt for building the Aswan Dam on the Nile, saying that excessive purchase of Communist arms had undermined Egypt's ability to pay. Egypt reacted by seizing control of the Suez Canal on July 26, 1956.

The Suez Canal had been dug, through Egyptian territory, under a concession negotiated in 1888, and was owned and operated by a corporation, the Universal Suez Canal Company, the stock of which was held largely in England and France. Egypt offered to pay for the stock at the prices of the day before the seizure, but that did not satisfy the users. Led by Britain, France, and the United

States, they tried to negotiate an acceptable agreement with Egypt, but without success, and on September 12, France and Britain complained to the Security Council. Negotiations were still under way when on October 29 the United States informed the Council that Israel had invaded Egypt in violation of the armistice. The U.S. called for an immediate meeting.

Israel charged that Egypt was building up its system of *fedayeen* raids not merely to harass but to destroy Israel, and that self-defense had made it necessary to seize the *fedayeen* bases.

On October 30, Britain and France called on Egypt and Israel to stop fighting and withdraw their forces ten miles from the Canal so as to avoid blocking traffic. They asked Egypt to agree to let them temporarily occupy the canal zone, which Egypt refused. In the Security Council the United States offered a resolution calling for a cease-fire and calling upon all members not to use force in the area. This was vetoed by Britain and France, and their aircraft began bombing military targets in Egypt the next day. The Security Council then called the Assembly into emergency session.

The Assembly met November 1 and urged that all parties agree to a cease-fire. The British and French, insisting on the necessity for police action, were willing to withdraw only if Egypt and Israel would consent to the sending of a United Nations force to keep the peace. On November 5 the Assembly voted to establish such a force, and it was assembled with great speed in the next few days, principally by air. Ten nations, none of them being among the Great Powers, provided the troops. Much of the transport and supplies were contributed by Italy, where the force was assembled, and by Sweden and the United States. The first unit of the UN Emergency Force was flown into Egypt on November 15.

At time of the cease-fire, Israel had captured most of the Sinai Peninsula, together with great stores of arms, and the Anglo-French forces had occupied the northern end of the Canal. As these forces withdrew the UNEF advanced, acting as a buffer to prevent contact between them and the Egyptians, until the UNEF came to rest along the Israeli border, where it settled down to the job of patrolling and preventing raids. It also took over from Israeli forces the forts on the narrow neck of the Gulf of Aqaba, which the Egyptians had previously used to block access to the Israeli port of Eilat, Israel's only door to the Far East.

The ships that had been sunk in the Canal were removed by contractors from Denmark and the Netherlands, with aid from other nations not involved in the conflict, working under UN auspices. The Canal was clear by the middle of April, 1957, and was opened for traffic, under the Suez Canal Authority which Egypt had created in July, 1956.

The net results of the flare-up in Egypt did not settle the conflicts between Israel and the Arab states or between Egypt and the users of the Suez Canal. Conditions in the Middle East remained highly explosive. But for the moment the influence of the United Nations, and the threat of Soviet intervention, had succeeded in quenching an outbreak that might have led to a much bigger war.

A by-product of the UN action was the invention of a new kind of police force, the UNEF. The Assembly made it clear that this force was not intended to take any part against one side or the other, but only to prevent "incidents" and renewed fighting. The questions in dispute must be left for negotiation, however long that might take. The central principle is that in the present explosive state of the world no actual shooting is allowable. Military power still has a large place in the negotiations of nations, but its use as a "deterrent" is accepted only as an unfortunate and dangerous necessity, to be mitigated if possible by disarmament. Meanwhile the UN does not recognize that any injustice or threat could justify starting a shooting war.

The UNEF was armed enough to stop a riot but not enough to resist an attack by an organized military force. Its defense was entirely moral. Any of the four contending nations that would attack a unit of the UNEF would be shooting the "soldiers of peace," as they were called. These were men from Brazil or Finland, India or Yugoslavia, who had come there to stand together in the line of fire so that no one could shoot at an enemy without killing a friend. As it worked out, even the civilian population treated the UNEF soldiers as friends. There were few signs of riot, and they soon disappeared. The moral protection worked.

In fact, UNEF has proved so useful along the Israeli-Arab border that it is hard to see when it can be withdrawn. In 1959 the Secretary-General reported to the General Assembly that conditions remained generally quiet, but if it were to be brought home there might be dangerous outbreaks. The force had been cut down as far as was safe, but it seemed to be a long-term enterprise that would require some more dependable method of financing than "assessments" that too often were not being promptly paid.

The UNEF is surely not all the world needs for keeping the peace, especially as such a force cannot even enter a fighting zone unless the belligerents first agree to a cease-fire. And there are still underlying conflicts of nations that must either be settled or lived down through the passage of time, if war is to be avoided. But every example of peacemaking is one step toward a more peaceful world. The UNEF is an invention that may find uses in future areas of tension.

The UNEF experience served as a valuable guide in mid-1960 when the Republic of the Congo, which attained independence on June 30, was confronted with a mutiny of sections of its troops against their Belgian officers, which spread to widespread attacks on Europeans in the territory. Belgium, the former administering authority in the Congo, intervened with troops to protect its nationals and others. The Congo accused the Belgians of "aggression" and appealed to the United Nations for military assistance, which the Security Council, meeting in urgent session, authorized the Secretary-General to provide. At the same time it called on Belgium to withdraw its troops. Meanwhile, the departure of Belgian technicians and administrative personnel left the country ill-equipped to run the machinery of government and keep its economy going. For the most part, the Congolese were without education and all technical and administrative experience. The result, complicated by the military situation, was chaos.

The Congo is one of the richest underdeveloped areas in the world. In the nineteenth century, a collapse of this kind would have brought in the European colonial powers to restore order, divide up the territory, and establish colonial administrations. But the world of 1960 could not endure any such intervention, especially since the Soviet Union and the United States would inevitably have been involved.

As Walter Lippmann, the great political commentator, observed, no practical cure for this dangerous crisis could be imagined without the United Nations, which "would have to be invented if it did not already exist." Even that would have offered poor prospects of success, in comparison with the use of the present going concern with its fifteen years of stormy experience back of it.

Mr. Lippmann pointed out that by the genius of Dag Hammarskjold, the Secretary-General, the UN force sent to the Congo was "not an international force as such and theoretically for all occasions, but a specialized force tailored exactly with tact and ingenuity to the situation. . . ."

This UN force drew its soldiers mainly from other African nations, a striking example of one of the values of regional handling of some kinds of problems. Food and supplies could safely be sent in from other regions, particularly from the Soviet Union and the United States. In the long run the UN force would be expected to serve as the channel for training and technical assistance to bring the new nation to a point where it can stand on its own feet.

In Walter Lippmann's words: "This UN enterprise is the most advanced and the most sophisticated experiment in international cooperation ever attempted. Among all that is so sad and so mean and so sour in world politics, it is heartening to think that something so good and so pure in its purpose is possible. No one can say that the experiment will succeed. But there is no doubt that it deserves to succeed."

Arab Refugees

In November, 1948, the General Assembly authorized a loan of $5,000,000 for the immediate relief of the Arabs who had fled from Israel, and urged the nations to make up a fund of $32,000,000 for the next ten months. The United Nations Relief for Palestine Refugees (UNRPR) was established, and received contributions of $35,000,000 from 33 governments. There were about 900,000 refugees to be cared for at that time.

A year later the Assembly decided to try a program of work relief—road building, forest planting, and other enterprises—that might open up new industries in which the refugees could become self-supporting. A Relief and Works Agency (UNRWA) was created, with Henry R. Labouisse of the U.S.A. as Director. Its work was hampered by the refusal of the Arab states to accept the refugees as permanent settlers, and their demand that Israel take them back. Israel's position was that to admit so many Arabs would endanger the country but that she was willing to discuss paying them for the lands from which they had fled. The refugees themselves remained as a dangerous source of unrest, especially in areas such as the Jordan Valley on Israel's eastern border.

Some little progress was made in the first ten years. By 1959, although there were now over a million refugees registered with UNRWA, many thousands not registered or drawing assistance from that organization were living and working in various parts of the Arab world. About 40 per cent of the refugees were living in camps built mainly with refugee labor. UNRWA was able to report that the vocational training programs and the loans for workers to set up small enterprises of their own were both "highly successful and are accepted by the refugees and the local governments," but funds were too limited and there were long waiting lists, a cruel example of having to save at the spigot and waste at the bung. UNRWA is assisted in its work by more than thirty international or foreign voluntary organizations and—an encouraging point—by a large number of small local groups in the host countries.

A proposal for a Jordan Valley Authority was put forward by Dr. Walter Lowdermilk of the U.S. Soil Conservation Service after World War II. The development of the Jordan River would supply water to irrigate much of the land in the district that is suitable for farming, and would provide jobs for hundreds of thousands of the refugees in the Arab parts of the valley. The benefits to be had by all concerned from loyally working together on this project would offer good reasons for keeping the peace. A successful Jordan Valley Authority, if established, might well stand as a good example of a practical instrument that might be used in other places where national interests overlap a territory that is rich in possibilities for united development.

The relations between France and Tunisia were established by a treaty in 1881 and a further agreement in 1883, which made Tunisia a French protectorate, although the Bey of Tunis remained as head of the Tunisian state. But in later years the Tunisians accused the French of moving in on them and taking full control of their affairs. In April, 1952, eleven Asian and African members of the UN joined in urging the Security Council to take up "the present grave situation in Tunisia."

The eleven members said that the French Resident-General had arrested the Tunisian Prime Minister and other members of the Cabinet, and that the controversy was a danger to peace. The French said that the officials had paralyzed the government and had to be removed so that the Resident-General could talk with the Bey in a suitable "atmosphere." The Council was unable to agree about what to do.

The eleven states, joined by two more, asked the Assembly to consider the question of Tunis. France declared that under the Charter the UN had no right to discuss Tunisia because it was a matter internal to France. The French delegation boycotted the meetings. Finally, the thirteen states joined in voting for a resolution proposed by eleven Latin American states. The resolution expressed confidence that France would help to develop free institutions in Tunisia, and the hope that the parties would continue negotiations to bring about self-government. A resolution to this effect was finally passed, 44 to 3, with 8 abstaining. A number of the members agreed with France that the question was domestic and should not have been discussed.

In this dispute, there was a split between the anti-colonial nations of Asia and Africa on one side and the colony-holding nations of Europe on the other. The American nations took a middle ground, trying to reduce the split by urging France to promote self-government.

Each year from 1952 on the Assembly discussed the Tunisian question and France continued to claim that the UN had no right to discuss it. France declared that on its own responsibility it would fulfill its promises to allow the Tunisians to manage their own affairs. Negotiations, in fact, resulted in an agreement signed on March 20, 1956. Tunisia became an independent nation and was admitted to the UN, along with Morocco, on November 12, 1956.

The neighboring territory of Algeria, however, remained in an unsettled state of rebellion against French control.

Czechoslovakia

In March, 1948, after the Communist revolution in Czechoslovakia, the Security Council considered a complaint by Dr. Jan Papanek, permanent UN representative from the old Czechoslovak Government. Dr. Papanek accused the U.S.S.R. of violating the independence of Czechoslovakia by a threat of force, and charged that the Soviets had helped directly and indirectly in the overthrow of his government.

The Soviet delegate denied the charges and said they had been brought up for the purpose of poisoning international relations and striking a blow at the United Nations. The new Government of Czechoslovakia refused to take part in the discussion, saying it was an interference in the country's internal affairs and contrary to the Charter.

Proposals to instruct a committee to look into the evidence were blocked by a Soviet veto. No results of any kind could be had in this case, and the Council, in the legal language of the report, "remained seized of the question."

Korea

The Korean outbreak was unique in several ways. The Republic of Korea had been endorsed by the UN, since the Assembly on December 12, 1948, declared that a lawful government had been established in South Korea. When, therefore, the North Korean forces crossed the 38th parallel on June 25, 1950 and invaded the Republic of Korea, the attack struck directly at the United Nations. If this attack had succeeded, the UN could be expected to fall apart as the League of Nations had done after it failed to act when the Japanese took Manchuria, Mussolini took Ethiopia, and Hitler took Czechoslovakia.

The second unique feature was the fact that the Soviet Union was boycotting the Security Council because it refused to give the Chinese seat to a delegate from Communist China. The Council was therefore able to act, in the absence of a Soviet veto, and it called into being a United Nations army to resist the invasion. This kind of resistance to aggression could of course never happen again, but it happened on this occasion and undoubtedly saved the United Nations from extinction.

As a result of the resistance of the ROK army and its UN allies, the invasion was eventually thrown back to the 38th parallel where it started and a truce was established.

Uniting for Peace

When the Assembly met in September, 1950, the need for some better arrangements to deal with future aggressions was plain. The original plan, adopted in 1945, was evidently not practicable under the conditions that had developed since that time.

The Charter originally provided for a UN police force, which many people hoped might in time grow to be stronger than any national military power. The police force was to be placed under the control of the Security Council, on which sat the Great Powers with their right of veto. It had to be assumed that all the Great Powers would stand against aggression, otherwise the UN system for enforcing peace by police power would of course break down. The idea of a world police force recalls the plan urged during World War I by William Howard Taft and other prominent citizens for a League to Enforce Peace— a forerunner of Mr. Wilson's proposal of the League of Nations.

Although the Security Council had never been able to agree on the organization of the UN police in Korea, it was suddenly possessed of a fighting force contributed by sixteen member nations. The command was delegated to the United States by action of the Council, and the Council symbolized its authority by raising the UN flag over the UN armies. Thus for once there was a UN force enforcing peace. But it could not happen again in any case where the Great Powers were not unanimous in their support. Something different would have to be tried.

The United States, therefore, brought into the General Assembly a set of resolutions called "Uniting for Peace." This proposal was discussed at length and finally passed on November 3, 1950, by 52 votes to 5, with 2 members abstaining. The 5 votes in opposition were those of the Soviet Union, Byelorussia, Czechoslovakia, Poland, and the Ukraine.

Under the new rule, if any sudden aggression breaks out, the Assembly can be called into emergency session on twenty-four hours' notice by any seven members of the Security Council in case the Council is blocked by a veto. Once the Assembly is in session, it can pass a resolution advising the member states of the emergency and calling upon them to help the victim by military and other means.

Since the Assembly is not always in session, it has established an Interim Committee to carry on when the Assembly is not sitting. The Interim Committee is made up of representatives of all the member states. One of its most important duties is to watch for dangers to the peace and to provide for calling the Assembly in an emergency.

In the Uniting for Peace resolutions the Assembly provided for a Peace Observation Commission, composed of representatives of fourteen states, including all the five permanent members of the Security Council. If trouble seems to be brewing along the border of any state, the Commission may send observers with that state's consent, so that the UN may get its own trustworthy reports on what happens. The Commission is at the service of the Interim Committee, the Assembly, and the Security Council.

Since any aggression is always launched with a barrage of false reports accusing the victim of being the aggressor, there might be confusion and delay in meeting the emergency if the UN did not have its own reliable source of information.

The adoption of the Uniting for Peace resolutions came only after a long and serious debate, in which the very nature of the United Nations was examined. The Soviet delegate, opposing the resolutions, said that they were designed to weaken the Security Council by taking away its full responsibility for peace and security.

The Soviet argument pointed out that the "principle of unanimity," that is, the veto, would be evaded if the Assembly could act when the Council was stopped by a veto.

The spokesmen for the resolutions said that under the Charter the Assembly had always had the right to express its opinion on any matter not being handled by the Council. In other words, the majority in the Assembly, by passing these resolutions, was asserting that the veto could block action only in the Council, but in so doing would leave the question free for consideration in the Assembly.

It should be said that the veto power was originally attached to the police power that was intended to be at the disposal of the Security Council. The United States insisted that if the UN was to have a police force it must be controlled by a body in which the United States could not be outvoted. All the other Great Powers felt the same way, since it was plainly impossible to have a peace organization attempting to discipline a Great Power by military force. The Uniting for Peace resolutions were not designed with any idea that the Assembly would organize a war against a first-class Power, i.e., would start World War III. They were designed to provide for suppression of a small or "brushfire" war in which no Great Power is prepared to fight openly on the side of the aggressor. That is what was done in Korea, but it was only an accident that the Security Council was able to act. Now the Assembly can act.

If any new war should flare up between small states or parties in a state, it may well be that the aggressor is secretly backed by one of the Great Powers, but that the backer, while prepared to veto any Security Council action, is not prepared to fight openly at the risk of a world war. In such a case the Assembly could promptly declare which side is the aggressor, and other Great Powers could then come in on the side of the victim, as several did in Korea, without necessarily starting World War III. It seems possible that since 1950 a number of brushfire wars in various parts of the world may have been prevented by this new ability of the Assembly to give an authoritative sanction to aid for the victim.

The flexibility of the UN is illustrated by the different uses that have actually been made of the Uniting for

Peace machinery. In the Suez crisis, the Assembly could not, of course, think of raising a force to fight against the two Great Powers that were engaged. But it met in emergency session, found that all the belligerents were willing to call off the fighting, and created an entirely new type of military force to police the armistice. In the Hungarian crisis no military operation under UN auspices was feasible but the Assembly was able to take a political action against the aggressor that would have been impossible in the Security Council.

Whether future crises can be successfully handled is of course impossible to say. But in Korea the United Nations not only escaped a mortal danger but also strengthened its constitution against future dangers.

The International Court

The International Court of Justice was established by a Statute which was made a part of the Charter. All members of the UN are "parties to the Statute," with voting rights in the choice of judges; and nonmembers can be admitted to the Statute on conditions laid down by the Security Council and the General Assembly.

Only states may be parties in cases before the Court, and only if they agree to submit to the Court's decision. Members can take their disputes before boards of arbitration or other tribunals of their own choice; but if they come into the Court they are bound to accept the Court's judgment.

A state may also declare that it promises in general to submit any and all questions of certain kinds to the Court, if an opposing state also agrees to the Court's jurisdiction. By 1958, thirty-eight states had accepted compulsory jurisdiction. The standard agreement covers all disputes about the interpretation of treaties, the application of international law, the existence of any fact that would be a breach of an obligation, and the amount of damages payable for the breach.

The Court is the successor to the Permanent Court of International Justice at The Hague. It is authorized to take jurisdiction in cases under old treaties that provided for the settlement of disputes by the former Court. The Court not only settles disputes between nations, but gives advisory opinions to the UN and its agencies on matters of international law or interpretation of the Charter.

The Court is made up of fifteen judges, no two from the same nation. They are elected as persons, not as representatives of their nations, by the Security Council and the Assembly voting separately without any veto.

If the Court does not include any judge of the nationality of a state that is a party to a pending case, that state is entitled to choose a person to sit as a judge for that case. This is contrary to the usual judicial principle by which a judge disqualifies himself from sitting in any case where he has a personal interest; it represents here a relic of the tradition of arbitration rather than judicial decision.

The Court has already decided a number of cases where the parties were in disagreement about the meaning of treaties or of international law.

One example was the dispute between the Government of Iran and the Anglo-Iranian Oil Company, in which the British Government appeared on behalf of the Company.

The Court ruled immediately that both parties should take no action to harm the property or prejudice the settlement while waiting for the Court to decide the dispute itself. Iran then gave notice that it withdrew its previous acceptance of the Court's compulsory jurisdiction. It also refused to accept the court's preliminary ruling. The question then before the Court was whether Iran could refuse the Court's jurisdiction without violating its treaty obligations. Iran appeared before the Court to argue its right to refuse to appear in the oil case.

The Court decided that Iran's original declaration accepting compulsory jurisdiction applied only to disputes about treaties signed after the date of the declaration. The records of debates in the Iranian Parliament and other evidence were brought in to establish that point. As no recent treaty covered the oil dispute, the Court declared that Iran was within its rights in refusing to argue the oil case before the Court. The United Kingdom had in the meantime complained to the Security Council about Iran's refusal to obey the preliminary ruling, but the question was settled by the Court's decision. Time therefore had to pass until the Iranian and British Governments finally came to an agreement between themselves.

At first glance it might seem that the Court accomplished little or nothing in the Iranian oil case. But as the oil question was not covered by any valid treaty rights, all the Court could do was to say so. It helped in the final pacific settlement of the dispute by rendering an authoritative judgment that Iran was not violating any rights coming under the Court's jurisdiction. This amounted to telling the parties not to accuse each other of bad faith but to make a bargain, which in the end they did.

In 1950 France and the United States came to the Court with a dispute about the rights of United States citizens in Morocco. The dispute covered a number of subjects and the decisions differed accordingly. The Court decided that United States citizens should have the same rights as French citizens to import goods free of certain currency controls. The claim of the United States that disputes between its own citizens should be tried in the United States Consular Courts, in both civil and criminal cases, was upheld. But the Court decided against the claim that a United States citizen in a dispute with a Moroccan could be tried by the consul, except in special cases covered by treaty.

In April, 1957, as a sequel to its seizure of the Suez Canal, the Egyptian Government deposited with the UN a declaration stating how it proposed to operate the Canal. It pledged itself to abide by the Convention of 1888 that established the international character of the Canal. In a later declaration, on July 18, Egypt formally accepted as compulsory the jurisdiction of the Court in all legal disputes that might arise over the interpretation of the Convention or other treaty provisions relating to the Canal.

In April, 1960, the Court finally ruled on the complex right-of-passage dispute between Portugal and India. The dispute concerned two detached bits of Portuguese territory in India, the villages of Dadrá and Nagar-Aveli, and their communication with the Portuguese port of Damão. Portugal had held the sovereignty over these villages since about 1800, with a right of access across Indian territory, subject, however, to Indian traffic controls.

In 1954, Indian armed bands took possession of the villages while the Indian authorities blockaded the roads. Portugal filed a complaint saying that India had prevented

Portuguese aid from reaching the villages, and accused India of a campaign to annex them. India replied that the "independent administration" that had been governing the villages since July, 1954, was mainly composed of natives or long-time residents of the villages, and that their nationalist sympathies had long been known.

The Court ruled by a vote of 11 to 4 that Portugal had the right of passage for civil officials, private persons, and ordinary goods. But it ruled, 8 to 7, that Portugal had no right to send military forces or arms and ammunition across Indian territory to the villages. And it ruled, by 9 to 6, that India had not violated the rights of passage legitimately belonging to Portugal.

International Law Commission

The General Assembly in 1947 created the International Law Commission to write a code of international law. The Commission started with a draft of a Declaration of the Rights and Duties of States. Rights include the right to political independence, to govern the state's territory and to fight in self-defense. Duties include keeping treaty promises, settling all disputes by peaceful means, refraining from using force without UN authorization, and respecting the basic rights of all citizens and aliens in the state's jurisdiction. At its 1949 session the Assembly recommended the draft to the attention of member states and asked for comments and advice.

The Commission was particularly asked to draft the principles of international law covering war crimes, as developed in the trials of Nazi war criminals at Nürnberg. It has also studied the principle of reservations which may be made by a nation at the time of ratifying an international agreement. The Commission suggested that future conventions should contain a provision making clear what would be the position in case of ratification with reservations.

Other questions studied by the Commission have included the possibility of defining aggression and of defining offenses against the peace and security of mankind. There is much difference of opinion among member states, not only as to exactly what acts would surely amount to aggression, but also as to whether it is safe to make a list of such acts. Some members fear that an aggressor, if provided with an exact list, would find ways of attack not positively included in the list, and so create confusion at the moment when the world should be uniting to resist what everyone knows to be an attack.

The Commission has prepared a draft of a code of arbitration procedures, and another for the international laws of nationality and statelessness. It has made studies of the possibility of setting up an International Criminal Court, to try people accused of international crimes such as genocide.

The 1956 session of the Commission was devoted mainly to a codification of the law of the sea. The Commission recommended a general international conference, at which many points not yet settled might be put in the way of international agreement. The General Assembly voted in February, 1957, to call such a conference for early in 1958. The program of the conference included such questions as the limits of the territorial sea, the right of innocent passage, fishing and oil-drilling rights on the continental shelf, the nationality of ships, penal jurisdiction in cases of collision, sea pollution, the slave trade, and piracy, including piracy by aircraft.

By developing international law, by settling some kinds of disputes in court, and by direct action in the Security Council or the Assembly to urge the nations to keep the peace, the UN has a long list of successes to its credit. Some disputes have been settled so completely that none of the parties concerned has any intention of bringing them up again. Some have merely been quelled, leaving both sides still enemies but not in a state of all-out war. Some of the disputes were of little consequence, since the parties were not likely to fight over the matter anyway, yet their settlement added to the orderly process of world association. Some disputes were important, because if they had flared up into heavy fighting the structure of world peace could have been dangerously undermined.

In all cases, settlements and judicial decisions help to build the framework for a peaceful world. Principles once established and then used in the decision of still other disputes gain respect. They stand as obstacles to future quarrels, cooling the blood of angry patriots who in the first flush of excitement may think they have more right on their side than later judgment will allow. All this work of conciliation, settlement, and definition, some of it too prosaic to make the front pages of the newspapers, is quietly building foundations upon which, if there is time, a solid world peace may someday be erected.

REGIONAL ARRANGEMENTS

According to the UN Charter, member nations may form regional alliances to maintain peace and security, provided these activities are "consistent with the Purposes and Principles of the United Nations." In 1945, when the Charter was adopted, the main purpose of this clause was to avoid disturbing the rapidly growing organization of the American republics, which had already come to be a force for peace and understanding in the Western Hemisphere. It was generally expected, however, that future disagreements among the UN members could be settled within the United Nations, and that there would not be much practical need for regional defense alliances. This expectation turned out to be premature.

Military alliances have grown up among the North Atlantic countries and the Western Pacific countries, in addition to agreements for strengthening the collective security of the American republics. Economic and political arrangements have also come into being in Western Europe looking toward some kind of federal European union. All these alliances and united agencies are designed to fortify the peace by military, economic, and political cooperation. They are auxiliaries to the United Nations. They cover areas smaller than the UN world-wide field of action—regions in which the nations have in common more principles and traditions of united action than are to be found in the broader society of the world as a whole.

NATO

The Western European and North American allies demobilized their armed forces as rapidly as possible after

World War II. Their people did not expect any further trouble that would call for large-scale military defense, and they wanted the boys home.

Later these nations became convinced that the Soviet Union had not demobilized on anything like the same scale. Five of the countries of Western Europe, therefore, decided to unite and build up their defense forces. Britain, France, Belgium, the Netherlands, and Luxembourg signed a Western Union defense treaty in Brussels on March 17, 1948. As soon as the news of this treaty reached Washington, President Truman welcomed the action and declared that the United States would be glad to help.

The United States Senate adopted on June 11 a resolution proposed by Senator Arthur Vandenberg recommending that the United States join in regional arrangements for collective security. With this backing, the President began negotiations with other countries in the North Atlantic area. These negotiations led to the North Atlantic Treaty, which was signed on April 12, 1949.

The twelve original members of the North Atlantic Treaty Organization, or NATO, were Belgium, Canada, Denmark, France, Iceland, Italy, Luxembourg, the Netherlands, Norway, Portugal, the United Kingdom, and the United States. Greece and Turkey joined in February, 1952.

The principal section of the Treaty is Article 5, in which the members pledge themselves to consider an attack on any one of them as an attack on all. Article 3 pledges the members to cooperate in increasing their defensive strength by self-help and mutual aid. In Article 2, the members promise to build up their free institutions and to avoid economic conflicts among themselves. The treaty provides in Article 7 that it shall not be so interpreted as to affect in any way the obligations of the members to the United Nations, and it recognizes "the primary responsibility of the Security Council for the maintenance of international peace and security." In case of sudden attack the NATO forces will act as may be necessary and will immediately report to the Security Council. If the Security Council is able to take the necessary measure, NATO will withdraw and leave the Security Council in sole charge.

In September, 1950, as part of the new thinking that resulted from the attack in Korea, the Council of NATO unanimously agreed to invite the West German Government to contribute armed forces for the common defense of Europe. Everyone was acutely conscious of the resemblance between divided Korea and divided Germany, and of the possibility that an attack might be made on Western Germany. In 1955, Western Germany was made a full member of NATO.

In 1956, the NATO Council appointed a committee to develop the nonmilitary aspects of the alliance. This committee, made up of the foreign ministers of Canada, Italy, and Norway, known as the "Three Wise Men," recommended close and frequent consultation among the members on their political and economic policies as new questions come up, before each nation has fully decided on its own position.

As a result of these recommendations, NATO has taken on some important political work, although it is not in any way a federal government. NATO is the chief political link between the United States and the Western European members, reflecting the traditional cultural ties among the peoples bordering on the North Atlantic. It has also been found to be a most effective agency for settling disputes between its own members, since all the other members take a keen interest in finding an acceptable way out. The bitter dispute between Britain and Greece over the island of Cyprus, and the dispute over fishing rights in the waters near Iceland, were worked out largely through the help of the NATO meetings. In the preparation for high-level conferences between the Western Powers and the Soviet Union, NATO provides a means through which all the members can express their views to the governments that will negotiate for the West.

European Union

The dream of a political union of Europe is as old as the Roman Empire. In modern times Hitler tried to unite Europe under his dictatorship. Among the free peoples of Europe the dream takes the form of a United States of Europe, with some kind of federal government. There are, however, many obstacles in the path of European union, ranging from ancestral hatreds to commercial trade barriers that powerful interests demand as protection against competition.

On the other hand, there are forces pushing the Europeans toward political union.

The most conspicuous pressure toward union is the necessity for common defense. Defense requires more than a unified military force. In the long run defense demands a great increase in the efficiency of European production. And that calls for political union.

In the United States one of the main reasons for high production per man-year is the political union of the states. Under the federal union, the states are forbidden to raise trade barriers against one another's products. Although this prohibition is often evaded, the evasions are of little effect compared with the customs barriers and the change of money between the states of Europe. Another advantage of the political union of the United States is that the Federal Government is strong enough to make and enforce laws against monopoly. These laws too are often evaded, but there is notably less monopoly in the United States than in Europe. Trade barriers and monopoly work together in Europe to waste the energy of the people.

In Europe, it has long been recognized that if the shackles could be loosened, production might be greatly increased. Military costs would be easier to bear. Living conditions would improve. European statesmen are well aware of the strong reasons for trying to build a United States of Europe.

The Council of Europe

After World War II, many organizations sprang up to promote one or another form of European union. In May, 1948, a general conference of Movements for European Unity was held at The Hague. The conference recommended that a European Assembly should be created. As a result, the five countries that had signed the Western Union Treaty at Brussels in March of that year decided to invite Italy, Ireland, and the three Scandinavian countries to join in forming a Council of Europe. The ten countries signed the agreement on May 5, 1949. Five others joined later.

The Council has not had much work to do, since there are so many other regional agencies in Europe. It has also suffered from the fact that there are two opposing views on European union. In general, the continental Europeans look for a close federal union with a strong government over all. Britain and the Scandinavian countries prefer a less formal cooperative alliance. Actual growth toward European union has taken place mainly in connection with economic agreements, rather than by direct attempts at political organization.

Benelux

An early move toward European union was the economic agreement of Belgium, the Netherlands, and Luxembourg, known as Benelux. This agreement was signed in 1944 by the governments in exile in London. It called for a customs union, to do away with tariffs among the three member states and to set up a single tariff wall to protect all three against imports from the outside. Its purpose was to enlarge the free trading area of the member countries and to create a combined economic system strong enough to compete in world trade. There were considerable differences, however, in cost and price of goods between Holland and Belgium, and many business concerns would have been ruined if trade were freed too suddenly of all obstacles. So although tariffs were abolished among the Benelux states, effective January 1, 1948, some trade quotas and currency controls were continued.

Meanwhile the members developed a new agreement, signed in 1947, to work toward a full economic union, one that would be able to stand the free flow of goods, investments, and people throughout the area. Full economic union would have to include a close interlocking of the economic, financial, and social conditions in the three countries, so as not to have such differences in levels as to cause a dangerous one-way flow in the channels of trade. All their foreign relations that affect these internal conditions must be carried on by the Benelux union rather than by the separate states.

Organization for European Economic Cooperation

OEEC was formed to coordinate the work of the European states in operating the Marshall Plan. The United States had announced in June, 1947, that if the Europeans would work out a coordinated plan for their own recovery the United States would contribute to help them pay the necessary costs. A temporary committee of sixteen European states drew up the plans for the new program. In 1948, as soon as the United States Congress had authorized the plan, the OEEC was established.

At first OEEC was busy with rebuilding the shattered industry and agriculture of Europe. This work made such progress that soon the Organization turned its attention to longer-range problems such as efficiency of production and the lowering of trade barriers.

By January, 1960, the prosperity of Western Europe had made such remarkable progress that a special economic committee met in Paris and recommended a general remodeling of the Organization. The chief purposes of the change were stated to be a broadening of economic and trade policies so as to continue the development of the member states, help in the growth of world trade, and cooperation in promoting the prosperity of the less-developed countries of the world.

In the earlier days, when the member countries often had trouble with foreign exchange problems, an important offshoot of the OEEC was the European Payments Union. A member country might find itself running a trade surplus with one neighbor and a trade deficit with another. In order to avoid having to restrict imports in an effort to prevent such deficits, the country could deposit its surplus foreign money in EPU and get credit in the other money it needed. As conditions improved, EPU was no longer needed, and it faded out in December, 1958. A branch of EPU, the European Monetary Agency, which makes loans to help a member stabilize its currency, is still operating and has aided Greece, Spain, and Turkey.

The Schuman Plan

This plan for a united political control over the steel and coal industries of Europe was proposed by Robert Schuman, the French Foreign Minister, in May, 1950. The treaty establishing the European Community for Coal and Steel was signed April 18, 1951, by France, the Federal Republic of Germany, Italy, Belgium, the Netherlands, and Luxembourg.

The purposes of the Schuman Plan were: first, to improve the efficiency of coal and steel production in Europe;

and second, to create a regional program of great economic importance in which France and Germany would work together as partners, and so might learn to forget old hatreds and become friends.

Efficiency was sought by enlarging the market area and by prohibiting monopoly practices. After a period of gradual adjustment, the trade barriers would disappear, and coal and steel could be shipped from one place to another inside the Community wherever the cost and price relationships called for them to go. This freedom would kill off the most inefficient producers and enlarge the operations of the more efficient ones. But it would not work if they should arrange a cartel or other monopoly scheme to prevent the free flow of trade.

The Community is authorized to forbid monopoly, and to fine any company that is convicted of practicing it. In order to exercise the power of enforcing an antimonopoly law, the Community is equipped with a real government, consisting of a High Authority of nine members, a Consultative Committee, an Assembly, a Council of Ministers, and a Court. The Court has power to reverse the decisions of other bodies in the Community for exceeding their authority. As a whole the Community is a true federal government, superior to the six member states, within the field of the laws governing coal and steel.

By 1957 the High Authority was able to report that practically all the old trade barriers had been removed. Steel production, which had been lagging before 1952, had increased 36 per cent in five years, considerably faster than that of Britain or the United States, though still slightly less than in the Soviet Union.

Meanwhile the Community was powerfully reinforced by the addition of two other organizations, the Common Market and Euratom.

The Common Market and Euratom

Three years after the establishment of the European Community for Coal and Steel, the Benelux nations proposed to France, Germany, and Italy the extension of similar agreements to cover trade in general and the development of atomic energy. The foreign ministers of the six countries met in June, 1955, and began discussions that led to the signing of two new treaties on March 25,

1957. One of these established the European Economic Community, known as the Common Market; and the other the Atomic Energy Community, or Euratom.

Each of these organizations was given a form similar to that of the Community for Coal and Steel, with separate executive commissions but with the same Assembly, Council, and Court acting for all three.

The transition to over-all free trade within the Community takes longer than for coal and steel because of the great number of different items, but it is planned to be completed in about fifteen years. The Community as a whole will have a single tariff law for imports from the rest of the world. Other European countries, however, will be welcome to join as full members or to come inside a free-trade area on special terms.

The treaty provides for numerous special organs to aid in economic development, such as a Monetary Committee and a European Investment Bank. For the time being the general budget will be carried by contributions from the member governments. But the Coal and Steel Community already has power to tax the industries under its control, and in time the Common Market organization will undoubtedly develop tax powers.

Euratom is similar in form but is comparatively simple because there are no great vested interests in atomic energy to be disturbed by the abolition of trade barriers. Euratom handles importation of atomic fuels, promotes research and training, helps private companies plan for building atomic power plants, sets standards for health and safety, and guards against use of atomic fuels for military or criminal purposes.

An agreement for cooperation was signed between Euratom and the United States on November 8, 1958. The United States guarantees a supply of enriched uranium for a ten-year development, at regular U. S. prices, and will share in the costs of the program. Technical knowledge supplied by the U. S. Atomic Energy Commission gives Euratom a start toward practical use of atomic power, which it would take many years to build up from the beginning. In return, the United States gets immediate experience in construction of large atomic power plants which would be wasteful in its own area in competition with cheap coal and oil but are needed in Europe where regular fuels are comparatively costly.

Both Euratom and the United States keep in close touch with the United Nations International Atomic Energy Agency, expecially on such problems as international control of dangerous nuclear materials.

The Seven

After the establishment of the Common Market by the six countries of the Coal and Steel Community, seven other European countries met in Stockholm in December, 1959, and signed an agreement for gradual reduction of tariff duties among themselves. The Seven are: Sweden, Norway, Denmark, the United Kingdom, Portugal, Switzerland, and Austria.

It is expected that the remodeled OEEC will have an important part to play in defining the relations between the two Western European economic communities, since OEEC includes most of the members of both.

The Western Pacific

The settlement of the war with Japan was not a responsibility of the UN, but of the fifty-four nations that had been on the winning side. In 1947, the United States proposed a peace conference, but the plan fell through because the Soviet Union refused to cooperate. Finally, in 1950, President Truman decided to go ahead and make peace if possible, even without the Soviets, He appointed John Foster Dulles to negotiate with Japan and with the Allies. The result was the Peace Conference at San Francisco in 1951 where the Soviet efforts to prevent the signing of the peace were unsuccessful. Japan signed the treaty with forty-eight other nations.

The attack in Korea and Chinese aid to the Communists in Indochina roused fears of a massive Communist drive against Southeast Asia and the islands of the Western Pacific. As a result of these danger signs, in 1954 Mr. Dulles, by then the United States Secretary of State, proposed a Pacific regional defense treaty somewhat like NATO. A conference was held in Manila in September.

The only Asian countries to take part were the Philippines, Thailand, and Pakistan. The other members of the Conference were Australia, France, New Zealand, the United Kingdom, and the United States. Many Asians were suspicious of these other partners in Asian defense, wondering if they might have imperialistic designs of their own. In order to meet these suspicions the Pacific Charter, adopted at the Conference, pledges all the members to promote the independence "of all countries whose people desire it and are able to undertake its responsibilities."

The Conference also adopted a Southeast Asia Collective Defense Treaty in which the parties agreed to unite in defense of any member subjected to attack, or of any other area that the members should unanimously agree to include in their common defense line. A protocol to this treaty specially mentioned Laos, Cambodia, and the non-Communist part of Vietnam, the three states of Indochina, as coming under the protection of the agreement, but stressing that the members would take action on the territory of these states only with their consent.

The treaty emphasized the duty of the members to cooperate not only in defense but in economic development, and there has been some modest but effective SEATO activity in this latter field. The bulk of the economic growth in the treaty area, however, has been based on aid from the United States; important help has also come from the United Nations and from the Colombo Plan.

The Colombo Plan is a regional agreement for technical assistance that was started by members of the British Commonwealth, but from the first it has welcomed other free Asian countries. It works in cooperation with the United States aid program and the technical assistance program of the UN. In economic problems as well as in those of collective security many Asian countries are struggling with conditions that invite aggression and that can be corrected only by a long process of upbuilding.

The Middle East

In order to guard the peace in the Middle East, several of the countries along the northern border decided to form a regional organization, and an agreement was signed on February 24, 1955, at Baghdad, Iraq, by Turkey, Iraq, Iran, Pakistan, and the United Kingdom. This agreement was known as the Baghdad Pact, but in 1958 Iraq, after a sudden revolution, ceased to take part in the organization. In 1959 the name was changed to Central Treaty Organization, or CENTO. The United States has from the first taken a keen interest in this organization, and is a member of several of its working committees.

Aside from the coordination of defense measures, CENTO has also begun to work toward more rapid development of the resources of the region. Mutual technical assistance is organized in agriculture, public health, and scientific research, and special emphasis is laid on transport and communications between the member states, which are separated by much mountainous and desert country. One of the first projects was a railway link between Turkey and Iran, avoiding the roundabout route through Soviet territory. Another was a microwave radio transmission system three thousand miles long—the longest in the world, from Ankara in Turkey to Karachi in Pakistan. CENTO is also cooperating with ICAO in supplying modern aids to air navigation through this difficult stretch of territory.

The Organization of American States

The regional organization of the Western Hemisphere has been a natural result of the liberation, more than a century ago, of groups of European colonies, born in weakness and needing the strength of union. First the English colonies after gaining their independence joined to form the United States. Then, in 1826, Simón Bolívar, the great Liberator of the Spanish colonies, called the First Congress of American States at Panama City. Delegates came from Columbia, Central America, Peru, and Mexico, and signed a "Treaty of Perpetual Union."

In the Monroe Doctrine (1823) the United States with the informal backing of British sea power warned the European Holy Alliance, led by Russia, not to try any new colonization in the Americas. For more than a century the Monroe Doctrine was a one-sided defense of the continent. The Latin American countries regarded the United States with suspicion, fearing that in warning the Europeans to keep out it was merely reserving the Western Hemisphere for its own imperialistic ambitions.

These suspicions were increased in the early years of the present century, when several Caribbean republics failed to pay their debts and the European creditors threatened to land soldiers to enforce payment. President Theodore Roosevelt feared that the Europeans, once ensconced, might decide to stay. He therefore decided to land United States forces and take over the collection of taxes until the debts were properly covered. The Latin American nations resented having the United States act as continental policeman.

President Herbert Hoover abandoned the intervention policy, and the feeling of the Latin Americans toward the United States began to improve. Further improvement of relations during the administrations of President Franklin Roosevelt and President Truman led to the formal establishment of the Organization of American States in 1948.

For many years there had been developing an organization of the American republics, originally designed for the promotion of commerce among the nations of the continent. The first meeting for this purpose was held in Washington in 1889–90, and others were held in later years at which the organization was gradually developed. It was governed by a Governing Board, made up at first of the U. S. Secretary of State and the Washington ambassadors of the other members, and later composed of special delegates chosen by the member countries. Its headquarters staff was called the Pan American Union, and was housed in a monumental building of that name in Washington.

In 1947 at Rio de Janeiro the American states signed the Inter-American Treaty of Reciprocal Assistance, which later served in part as model for the North Atlantic Treaty of 1949. At Bogotá in 1948 they adopted a new Charter establishing their association as the Organization of American States, with the Pan American Union as its secretarial body. The main assembly of the Organization, called the Conference, meets about every five years to settle general policies. A Council, formerly the Governing Board of the Pan American Union, manages the Organization's routine affairs.

Like the UN, the OAS has certain dependent agencies which give technical services to the members in economic, legal, and cultural fields. It also has a number of specialized organizations affiliated with it, such as the Pan American Institute of Geography and History, and institutes for the protection of women and children, and for the development of agriculture. These agencies are coordinated by the Pan American Union, and also cooperate with the corresponding agencies of the UN.

One of the most recent OAS affiliates is the Inter-American Development Bank, founded in April, 1959, to provide capital for private and public projects in the American republics.

The Pan American Sanitary Bureau, established in 1902, is the oldest international public health agency in the world. It now acts as secretariat of the Pan American Health Organization, which on one hand is a specialized agency of OAS and on the other acts as regional organization of WHO. The work of PAHO has been rapidly expanding until its budget has become larger than that of OAS. It works in three main fields: the fight against infectious diseases; general public health; and the education of health workers.

PAHO is promoting campaigns against malaria, smallpox, yellow fever, yaws, syphilis, polio, rabies, leprosy, and the plague. In these campaigns it works closely with UNICEF and the UN Technical Assistance program, as well as with United States agencies.

Immediately after the great earthquake in Chile in May, 1960, the Pan American Sanitary Bureau reported airlifting to the stricken country half a million doses of smallpox vaccine and other donated medicines, including gangrene antitoxin and various antibiotics.

The fight against yellow fever, for instance, has required the total extermination of the dreaded Aëdes Aegypti mosquito, which carries the city variety of the disease. This mosquito is now reported extinct in nearly a dozen countries from Panama to Uruguay. Jungle yellow fever is another problem.

The plague is carried by ground squirrels and other small wild animals in many American countries, including the United States. PAHO provides consulting experts to advise on control of these plague-carrying animals.

Another important health program has been the development of a special low-cost food for children in Central America, where undernourishment is widespread. The new food, called Incaparina, is a high-protein mixture of cottonseed meal, corn or rice, sorghum, calcium carbonate, yeast, and vitamin A. It is readily accepted by the children as well as the adults and produces extraordinary improvement in the health of children.

The Inter-American Institute of Agricultural Sciences is carrying on a series of experiments in the use of radio-

active materials in agriculture. A field near Turrialba,
Costa Rica, with banks of earth around it to control the
radiation, is planted with coffee, bananas, cacao, and
other crops to be bombarded with gamma rays, to stimulate the development of new varieties, some of which might
be of great value.

By-passing the UN

With new regional agreements being built up, a great
amount of negotiation goes on outside the UN. Friends
of the UN often criticize the Powers for "by-passing" the
UN, and express the fear that the UN may wither away.
The smaller nations in the Assembly are naturally concerned when the Great Powers discuss matters in special
conferences where the rest of the nations have no chance
to give their opinions or cast their votes.

On the other hand, Article 33 of the Charter directs
the members to try to settle their disputes first of all by
"negotiation, enquiry, mediation, conciliation, arbitration,
judicial settlement, resort to regional agencies or arrangements, or other peaceful means of their own choice." In
other words, you must try to avoid appealing to the UN
Security Council or the Assembly, but if all other attempts
at peaceful settlement fail, then come in and let the world
organization judge.

The question about by-passing is a common feature of
any system of organizations on more than one level. In
human affairs generally, some matters are settled by the
family, some by the village or town, some by a country or
province, others by a nation or by a regional group of nations or by the human race organized in the United Nations. The exact level where a problem is best handled is
often not clear. Continual disputes about "states' rights"
are a characteristic of federal governments; continual disputes about "domestic jurisdiction," nationalism, and regionalism may be expected in the UN.

The main principles for understanding such disputes
seem fairly clear.

Nationalism, for instance, is the feeling of a people that
they are by rights a nation and ought to have their own
"sovereignty." They feel oppressed if some other nation
rules them. The revolt against colonialism excites the feel-

ing of nationalism, now especially strong in Asia and Africa.

Nationalism is not a form of madness. If people have language, customs, and traditions in common they can settle many questions among themselves better than any other people can do it for them. They should be encouraged to do so, provided they do not disturb their neighbors too much.

Regionalism, in the same way, is the feeling of the nations in one part of the world that they have certain regional problems in common, and that they have some principles and standards in common that may outweigh their differences. Such feelings lead the nations to make regional agreements. This way of solving problems also makes sense provided the region does not form an alliance to conquer the rest of the world.

The United Nations is based on the feeling that all human beings are the same in some ways and therefore need an organization in which they can act as one on matters in which they agree as members of the human race. Such matters may include at least the desire to avoid total atomic desolation, and a general desire to promote some kinds of human rights and to raise the level of living. These are the general purposes of the vast majority of sane people. But whether some particular action is best planned on a world-wide scale or in some smaller unit depends on its special character.

The natural principles of human action in large or small groups are fairly plain. But the boundaries between one level of action and the next are apt to be hazy and clouded by the selfish interests of one nation or another. It is only to be expected that people will always argue about where the nation or the region leaves off and the proper field of the United Nations begins.

DISARMAMENT

The idea of an international agreement to reduce military forces was first proposed at a peace conference called by the Czar of Russia in 1899. Modern science was developing big guns and steel-clad warships, and these seemed so costly and dangerous that something would have to be done to put a limit on them. From then on the cost and danger have grown until the most advanced hydrogen and cobalt bomb offers the human race the possibility of killing all or nearly all the living things in the world by the poisoned earth and air left over from a short atomic war. The necessity of avoiding suicide is known to all the world, but how to do it is not so simple.

The Peace Conference of 1899 appointed a committee of experts to study the reduction of armies and navies. The committee reported that no agreement was possible at that time.

Another peace conference in 1907 agreed to prohibit the use of poison in war but did not try to agree on arms reduction.

After World War I the question was more urgent. The victorious Allies disarmed Germany, and decided to put a disarmament clause in the Covenant of the League of Nations which they were writing along with the peace treaty. Accordingly, Article 8 of the League Covenant provided that the League Council should make plans for arms reduction and offer them to the members for their signature. When these plans were adopted the members would promise to exchange "full and frank information on the scale of their armaments, their naval and air programmes and the condition of such of their industries as are adaptable to warlike purposes." A commission was appointed to advise the League on how to bring about the desired agreements.

In December, 1920, the commission advised that arms reduction at that time would be premature. A new commission was appointed in 1921, which came up with some further steps in the attempt to think out the disarmament problem.

The new principles, which the League Assembly accepted in 1922, were that no plan would work unless every nation joined, and that the nations must promise to help any country that might be attacked. Details of a proposed treaty of mutual assistance were brought forward in 1923. They included giving the League Council the authority to decide what forces each member should provide for the common defense. They also included the authority to judge, in case of an attack, which nation was the aggressor and which was the victim. The treaty would promise financial help to the victim and economic penalties against the aggressor.

By 1923, then, the main elements of a workable disarmament plan had been named, although naming them was far from being the same as getting the nations to agree to them. These are the main essentials:

1. Full disclosure. No country can have military secrets, or the other countries will be afraid to disarm.

2. Full membership. Every country big enough to be dangerous must be a member of the agreement.

3. Collective security, as it is now called. If any country is attacked the others must be bound by a promise to give immediate help without further argument.

4. Judgment. Some recognized authority must have the information and the means to give an immediate judgment saying which nation is the attacker and which is the victim.

All the arguments since 1923 have consisted of repeating the demand for these essentials in one form of words or another, and finding that some country was determined to leave out some necessary feature. Since that would open a loophole through which an aggressor might draw a sudden bead on his innocent victim, the insistence on the loophole has naturally led to disagreement.

After 1923 the nations of Europe saw little hope that the world could soon agree on a disarmament treaty. As a stopgap they tried regional peace agreements, such, for instance, as the Locarno Pacts. But in 1932 a great conference of sixty-one nations met at Geneva. In addition to fifty-six League members, the United States and four other nonmembers were there.

The Geneva Conference agreed on prohibiting certain weapons such as bombs dropped from airplanes or balloons. It agreed on the principles of arms limitation, of international supervision of the arms business, and of publicity of arms budgets. But it did not find a practical way to get the nations to act on these principles.

Soon afterwards, Japan and Germany resigned from the League of Nations. Then in 1935, when Germany started drafting men for its new army, the League gave up trying to promote disarmament. Hitler was planning conquest. For the time being it was too late for anyone to disarm.

It is sometimes said that it takes two to make a quarrel. This saying is true of nations only provided there are no aggressors. It takes only one nation to march over the border for the purpose of conquering its neighbors. So long as anyone who loves freedom has the means of resistance, there will be war if any one nation starts a military aggression.

On the other hand, if all the freedom-loving nations of the world were so completely disarmed that they could offer no resistance, an aggressor could take them over without a war. This is what the aggressor nations mean by their love of peace. Hitler, for instance, spoke often of his deep desire for peace, meaning that when he decided to march he hoped there would be no resistance. Aggressors are strongly convinced that it takes two to make a quarrel, and that if any nation resists their aggression that nation is a warmonger and is guilty of all the blood of those who suffer.

In 1935, when Hitler was building up his armies and talking of his love for peace, the other nations were afraid of what he might be planning to do. They were too much disturbed to disarm, though at the time not enough disturbed to start a heavy rearmament program. It will always happen that if the peace-loving Powers believe that any strong Power is dreaming of military conquests, they will be afraid to disarm and may on the contrary build up their armaments.

What use, then, is there in talking about disarmament year after year, and conference after conference, when everyone knows there are unspoken conditions in the argument that make it hopeless? The use is in the fact that conditions change, and the long years of discussion will help to bring on the needed change, if war should be postponed long enough.

By talking, the nations make clear to themselves and to any possible aggressor the necessary terms of peace and of disarmament as they are now understood. Much of the work of describing these necessary terms was done before 1923, but many details are still not clear. Some details may be less necessary than others. They might be sacrificed in bargaining, to save the face of a nation that is suspicious and reluctant to yield on more essential points. No free nation wants to demand or to endure any more international control than is really necessary to get the result. Long and seemingly hopeless argument is hammering out the terms that some day may be accepted.

What would make any aggressor willing to accept conditions that would forever disarm his power to conquer his neighbor? This is the key question of the mid-twentieth century. It has several answers.

If any leaders who want to conquer the world should be convinced that the devastation of a war would leave them in worse condition than they are now, a pressure would be set up in their minds toward giving up the dream of a short, easy, victorious war.

When the leaders who dream of conquest try to lull their victims by talk of peace and fail to get the victims to disarm, their confidence is temporarily shaken, and they show it by being unusually polite. If this condition continues a long time, if the free nations continue powerfully armed, the dream of conquest may gradually fade. Then the practical advantages in agreeing to a real disarmament may begin to appeal to men who had previously neglected them.

This principle can be easily illustrated by a bit of history that is now too old to carry any hard feeling. About a thousand years ago the Norsemen found profit in raiding the coasts of Britain. Sometimes they were successful, and sometimes the inhabitants killed them and nailed their hides to the church doors. In those days any agreement for a lasting peace would have seemed impossible. But as time went on, military raids on the British coasts ceased to be profitable adventures, and the Scandinavians forgot the whole idea. There is no raider so fierce that he may not quiet down if he finds there is no profit in the business.

Another reason for hope is the well-known fact that subversion in our time is a powerful technique of conquest. All modern aggressors count more or less on persuasion, the technique of the big lie, and the use of dupes for infiltration of the victim's institutions. The peace-loving nations that hope to resist aggression also count heavily on subverting the power of aggression by campaigns of truth. One of the best hopes of military peace is the belief on each side that it has a chance to win by propaganda, undermining the other side's will to resist.

Propaganda is cheaper and safer than shooting. Any aggressor who has a deep faith that he can win the world by propaganda and subversion would be glad to do it in that inexpensive way instead of by the simpler but more risky use of armed force against well-armed opponents.

If that be true, the hope of forever postponing a new world war and in the end of abolishing aggressive weapons is that much better than it was in 1935.

UN and the Atom Bomb

The UN Charter authorized the Security Council to make plans for the regulation of armaments and submit them to the members. The Assembly was also authorized to "consider the principles governing disarmament," and to make recommendations about them to the members.

Then a few weeks after the signing of the Charter the atomic bomb came into action, and the disarmament question was stepped up to a consideration of the life or death of the human race.

On November 15, 1945, Canada, the United Kingdom, and the United States proposed a UN commission to study the control of the atom. In December the Soviet Union joined in sponsoring the proposal. It was adopted unanimously at the first session of the General Assembly in January, 1946, and the Atomic Energy Commission was established, consisting of all members of the Security

Council together with Canada when not a member of the Council.

The Atomic Energy Commission soon became deadlocked. The U.S.S.R. would not allow unlimited inspection, saying that it infringed national sovereignty. It also demanded an agreement to abolish atomic weapons as a first step toward the adoption of a control system. The Western Powers insisted that safeguards against cheating were the necessary condition for any disarmament agreement.

In December, 1946, the General Assembly recommended that the Security Council make plans for reducing ordinary armaments. It also recommended an early start toward organizing the UN police force as provided in the Charter. At that time it was commonly believed that collective security, a necessary base for general disarmament, could be had by organizing UN armed forces to overawe any aggressor.

The Commission for Conventional Armaments was established by the Security Council in 1947, but it too bogged down. The Assembly abolished both commissions and in January, 1948, created a new Disarmament Commission with the same membership as the Atomic Energy Commission, to consider both atomic and ordinary arms restriction together. This body also became deadlocked over whether to start with an inspection system.

In July, 1955, President Eisenhower and the heads of the British, French, and Soviet governments held a "summit meeting" in Geneva, and arranged for a conference of their foreign ministers to take place in October. No final agreement resulted from either of these meetings.

The Disarmament Commission reported to the Assembly in November, 1955. The chief point of progress was agreement by the Soviet Union to the establishment of control posts in its territory and unlimited right of the control organization to inspect. But a serious stumbling block had arisen, the disclosure—agreed by all parties— that there was no known way of detecting hidden stores of atomic weapon materials, such as plutonium.

The Commission made little progress during the next year, for the Western Powers could not agree to the Soviet demands for immediate prohibition of nuclear weapons and the liquidation of all military bases in foreign states.

In 1957 there was some discussion of the possibility of partial disarmament as a first step, but no agreement was reached. Some progress, however, had been made. In that year the General Assembly urged the Powers to reach an early agreement to stop nuclear arms testing. It also urged them to halt the production of fissionable material for weapons, to cut down their stocks of such weapons, to proceed with general disarmament under proper safeguards, and to study how the use of outer space might be limited to peaceful purposes.

The United States, Britain, and the Soviet Union all voluntarily stopped the testing of atomic and hydrogen bombs, which had begun to spread measurable quantities of radioactive fallout. Meanwhile long and patient discussions were going on at Geneva on many technical problems that would have to be handled in any successful disarmament plan. There was, for instance, an attempt to agree on how to prevent surprise attack. There were long and encouraging talks on the cessation of nuclear tests, leading to an agreement that the obligation to stop the tests and the establishment of the control systems must go hand in hand. Britain and the United States dropped their insistence that the test ban should be continued year by year and made dependent on progress toward general disarmament; they agreed with the Soviets that tests would be permanently banned, so long as no one broke the agreement. There was a broad coming together on the general shape of a control organization, to be headed by a seven-nation commission. The negotiators agreed on the principle that nuclear explosions for peaceful purposes could be allowed under carefully prescribed conditions and under international observation. Many noncontroversial clauses for a proposed treaty were drafted; it was agreed that the treaty would come into force when ratified by the United Kingdom, the United States, and the U.S.S.R., but would be open to all nations with the hope of making it world-wide.

During 1958 and early 1959 evidence gradually piled up that the Atomic Powers were becoming more and more anxious about the growing danger of world suicide, and more serious in wanting to stop the arms race.

Finally on September 7, 1959, the UN representatives of Britain, France, the Soviet Union, and the United States sent a joint letter to the Secretary-General, notifying him that the four Powers had organized a new ten-member disarmament committee, consisting of equal numbers of socialist and nonsocialist states. The other six members were: Bulgaria, Canada, Czechoslovakia, Italy, Poland, and Romania.

The four Powers acknowledged that according to the Charter, "disarmament matters are of world-wide interest and concern. Accordingly, ultimate responsibility . . . rests with the United Nations. The setting up of the disarmament committee in no way diminishes or encroaches upon the United Nations responsibilities in this field. In setting up this committee, the special responsibility resting on the great powers to find a basis for agreement is taken into account."

The four Powers promised that the new committee would report its discussions to the UN Disarmament Commission, and arrangements were made to use the UN services and facilities in Geneva.

On September 10 the Secretary-General called a meeting of the Disarmament Commission, which had meanwhile been enlarged to include all the UN members, under a resolution passed in 1958. The Commission unanimously voted to welcome the resumption of negotiations, and expressed the hope that the ten-nations committee would find a useful basis for United Nations action.

The next development came on September 18, when Mr. Nikita Khrushchev, who was visiting the United States, addressed the General Assembly of the United Nations.

The Soviet leader proposed a four-year program of complete and general disarmament. He called for the total abolition of all armies, navies, and air forces, of general staffs and war ministries, and the closing of all military establishments, the destruction of all nuclear weapons, and the use of rockets only for peaceful exploration of outer space. He said the Soviet Union would be prepared to join with other nations in economic aid to the underdeveloped countries.

Mr. Khrushchev also declared that if the other Powers were not ready to embark on total disarmament, his government would be glad to agree on partial steps in that direction.

The General Assembly's Political and Security Committee began a full-scale discussion of disarmament on

October 9, 1959, which continued until November 2, during which time sixty-five nations presented statements on the subject, and two formal declarations were considered, one from the United Kingdom and the other from the Soviet Union.

The British proposed a three-stage disarmament that would eliminate all weapons of mass destruction and reduce armed forces "to levels which will rule out the possibility of aggressive war."

In the first stage the nations would study the test ban and the technical means for preventing the use of fissionable material in weapons; they would agree on limitation of their armed forces and certain kinds of armaments would be handed over to an international control body. There would be conferences on prevention of surprise attack, peaceful uses of outer space, and the formation of international control organs.

The second stage would see a progressive reduction of conventional weapons and forces; production of atomic weapon material would be cut off; stocks of atomic weapons and material would be reduced under a control system; and an inspection system to prevent surprise attack would be established. The Powers would agree on the use of outer space and on an international control organ.

In the third and last stage there would be comprehensive disarmament by all countries, under effective international control. The manufacture of nuclear, chemical, biological, and other weapons, would be prohibited. Use of outer space for military purposes would be forbidden. Stocks of mass-destruction weapons would be finally eliminated. International controls would be fully organized, including control over military budgets, and armed forces would be cut to the number required for internal security.

The Soviet four-year disarmament program would start with manpower reductions, under appropriate controls, cutting the armed forces of the United States, the Soviet Union, and Communist China to 1,700,000 men each, and those of the United Kingdom and France to 650,000 each; reductions in other states would be proportional.

The second stage would be the complete disbandment of armed forces, including the withdrawal of those stationed abroad.

In the third stage all nuclear weapons, missiles and

air force equipment would be destroyed, together with all stockpiles of material for chemical and bacteriological warfare. Scientific research for military purposes and all military education and training would be prohibited, and all military organizations would be abolished.

The budgets previously devoted to military purposes would be used for tax reductions, subsidies, and aid to underdeveloped countries.

An international control organ would be established to oversee the progress of disarmament and to act permanently as a guard against secret arming.

During disarmament states would maintain the ratio among their various armed services. That is, they would not start out by reducing the infantry and hanging onto all their ballistic missiles.

Any accusation of a violation of the agreement would be submitted to the United Nations.

In the debate the British representative pointed out with pleasure that on several points the Powers were clearly coming closer together. He noted that the Soviet Union no longer insisted on starting with abolition of nuclear weapons before making a start on the reduction of conventional forces. Another was the Soviet willingness to let the foreign bases remain until the end of the reduction of conventional forces. He reported that the test-ban conferences in Geneva had brought concessions from both sides and made substantial progress, though there was still some difference of opinion over how much inspection would be needed. He concluded by saying that prospects for agreement seemed better than at any time since the war.

The Soviet delegate praised the spirit of the Western delegates with whom he had negotiated the joint resolution to be presented by the Committee for Assembly action, saying, "Our partners demonstrated a constructive spirit which permitted a businesslike approach."

Henry Cabot Lodge, United States delegate, summed up his country's attitude toward disarmament as follows:

The United States "unreservedly supports, and has always supported, the greatest possible amount of controlled disarmament. . . . Adequate and timely inspection and control must be built into the system." He awaited further information on what inspection and control the Soviet Union would be willing to accept.

A point often made in the debate, especially by the smaller nations, was their pleasure at the thought of economic development taking the place of the arms race, as well as their insistence that the Big Powers were responsible for finding a way to avoid universal destruction.

Finally the Political and Security Committee recommended that the Assembly transmit the British and Soviet plans to the ten-nation committee for detailed study. This action was taken by the Assembly on November 20, in a unanimous vote.

As the 1959 session of the Assembly ended, there was a general feeling that disarmament was not as hopeless as it had appeared during the first twelve years after World War II.

But with the collapse of the summit meeting in May, 1960, international attention turned to the Soviet charges against the United States in the Security Council. The U.S.S.R. asked the Council to condemn as "aggressive acts" incursions by United States aircraft over the territory of other states and to call on the United States "to halt such actions and to prevent their recurrence." Instead, the Council adopted a resolution calling for continued negotiation to settle international issues. It appealed to all governments to refrain from the use or threat of force and "to respect each other's sovereignty, territorial integrity, and political independence." It also urged continued efforts toward disarmament.

On May 19, Secretary-General Dag Hammarskjold emphasized the need for continued work toward solving the problems that had been scheduled for discussion at the summit meeting. He pointed out that the responsibilities of the United Nations had been increased by the discouraging experiences in the use of other means. He expressed the hope that all member nations, great and small, would make use of the United Nations to overcome the setback which might otherwise "tie us down for a long time ahead."

OUTER SPACE AND THE ATOM

The principle that friendship among people of alien cultures is most readily built by working in cooperation for some valuable material achievement, may well find an important application in the exploration of space. Here the human race can look out upon something vast, cold, and unapproachable except through the gates of abstract science. If we can begin here with reverential awe, we can hope to continue with a growing sense that in the face of this majesty all human disputes are insignificant.

The danger that space exploration would focus on a contest between the Soviet Union and the United States for military advantage could be avoided only if the two antagonists could agree at an early stage that cooperation was the better way. The United Nations provides the meeting ground for the first stages of such an agreement which if achieved could be one of the greatest successes of its first fifteen years.

In December, 1959, the General Assembly debated the subject of outer space for the first time, and adopted without a dissenting voice a resolution creating the United Nations Committee on the Peaceful Uses of Outer Space, made up of twenty-four nations, conspicuously including the Soviet Union and the United States.

The main purposes of this Space Committee, as set forth in the resolution, are to promote international cooperation, and in particular to encourage the nations to carry forward on a permanent basis the space research begun with such cordial world-wide cooperation in the International Geophysical Year. The Committee is directed to encourage the nations to study space problems and exchange scientific information.

In addition, the Space Committee is to "study the

144

nature of the legal problems which may arise from exploration of outer space." No one knows much about what these problems will be, but anyone can see that near the earth, traffic control and allocation of radio bands will soon need to be considered by some international agency. In fact, the International Telecommunication Union announced in 1959 the formation of a committee to study the allocation of radio bands for space research. The committee was made up of representatives of Czechoslovakia, France, the U.S.S.R., the United Kingdom, and the United States.

If the Space Committee turns out to be an important means for pulling the world together, it will itself be one of the highest "peaceful uses of outer space." If so, the effect will develop gradually over a period of time, provided the existing tensions can be kept below the boiling point long enough for the peacemaking forces to take effect. In the meantime, the discussion that led up to the unanimous vote was in itself a peacemaking exercise.

Henry Cabot Lodge, of the United States, pointed out that the breakthrough into outer space was a challenge to the political as well as the scientific inventiveness of man. Outer space could not belong to any nation. Mr. Lodge called attention to the fact that many possible uses for space cannot be exploited except through world-wide cooperation—the material necessity that chiefly underpins the hope of such cooperation as a basis for peace. As man entered the field of outer space, he declared, a new perspective was created, and national boundaries and rivalries receded in importance. He was gratified that after weeks of patient negotiations, agreement had been reached with the U.S.S.R., and he welcomed the Soviet proposal for an international conference on outer space technology. Mr. Lodge concluded by saying that mankind had an unprecedented opportunity here, and urged, "Let us rise to the occasion."

Vassily V. Kuznetsov, of the Soviet Union, spoke of the need for international cooperation, not only to prevent extravagant waste of materials and manpower, but to make use of all the possibilities for progress. He spoke with pride of the Soviet cooperation in the International Geophysical Year program. He pointed out the need for continuing to accumulate a vast number of scientific observations before anything like an exact picture of the natural laws that apply in space can be obtained. His country would supply information to the scientists of the world as fast as it became available.

Mr. Kuznetsov also noted with satisfaction that in the negotiations leading up to the resolution the Soviet suggestions had been met with understanding. He said that a mutual desire to reach agreement had made it possible to work out the draft of the resolution.

The Soviet representative joined in emphasizing the peacemaking character of the proposed UN action, calling it a great step forward on the road to the development of international cooperation in the peaceful uses of outer space. At the same time, he declared, it would help to create a favorable atmosphere for the solution of other outstanding international problems in the interests of strengthening world peace.

There were enthusiastic speeches by the British, French, Australian, and Japanese representatives. Jerzy Michalowski, of Poland, paid tribute to the spirit of conciliation shown by the United States and the Soviet Union in their negotiations, and expressed deep satisfaction with the peaceful atmosphere in which the Fourteenth Assembly was closing. He noted that the space age had found mankind unprepared for what would need to be done in this field, but that the International Geophysical Year had shown the way to fruitful international cooperation.

Chandra Shekhar Jha, of India, called the agreement between the U.S.S.R. and the United States "another milestone in progress," and observed that progress would have to be made toward ensuring that outer space was not used in any way for military purposes.

Wallace P. Nesbitt, of Canada, pointed out that there were large areas of space research that in the end must be covered by the United Nations itself, since there would be a need for rules and regulations that could be established only by the UN. One aspect of space law, he said, should be immediately recognized—that no land on the moon or any planet could belong to any nation.

In this historic discussion, for the moment at least, all the delegations seemed to feel a cool breath of fresh air and the possible dawn of peace. All the nations, great and small, gave a sigh of relief, for though the danger of universal madness and suicide had not been abolished, human sanity had broken through in a new direction that could be a path to peace.

With this breakthrough the importance of the United Nations itself rose to a new level. In particular, the feeling long held by many friends of the UN, that in the end that body must be sovereign of the open spaces of the world —the high seas, the South Polar Continent and even the interoceanic canals—broke through into the sky with the Canadian hint of UN sovereignty in outer space.

Peaceful Uses of the Atom

On December 8, 1953, President Eisenhower addressed the General Assembly of the United Nations. He called attention to the dangers of total destruction by atomic and hydrogen bombs, and suggested a new "Atoms for Peace" plan for easing the suspicions that were preventing agreement on controls.

The President proposed that the Powers having nuclear materials contribute some of them to a pool to be used for the peaceful development of atomic energy. He suggested that the program should be operated by an International Atomic Energy Agency, to be sponsored by the United Nations.

The Soviet Union agreed to negotiate with the United States on the matter but wanted to combine the President's proposal with a ban on atomic weapons, one of the main points of dispute in the disarmament negotiations. It also wanted the new agency to be controlled by the Security Council, where it would be subject to the veto. The United States insisted on keeping it free of such entanglements.

On December 4, 1954, the Assembly unanimously adopted a resolution endorsing the proposed International Atomic Energy Agency and calling for an international conference to study how the peaceful uses of atomic energy might be developed by cooperation among the nations. In 1955 a world conference on the peaceful uses of the atom was held in Geneva. The proceedings of the conference and the papers submitted by the world's leading scientists who attended were afterwards published by the United Nations in sixteen volumes. In 1956 representatives of the twelve nations that already had some atomic resources met from February to April in Washington.

The founding statute of the Agency, which includes a provision for inspection to make sure that stocks of nuclear fuel provided by the Agency would not be used for making weapons, was signed by eighty nations in October, 1956. Sterling Cole, of the United States, was appointed Director-General of the Agency. The IAEA opened for business on October 1, 1957, at its headquarters in Vienna. To set it on its way the United States pledged 5,000 kilograms (about 11,000 lbs.) of uranium 235, the Soviet Union pledged 50 kilograms, and other members smaller amounts. Much larger quantities would of course be used every year after the program got fully under way.

The Second International Conference on the Peaceful Uses of Atomic Energy was convened by the United Nations in Geneva in 1958. More than two thousand papers on atomic science submitted by nuclear authorities of forty-six countries and six intergovernmental agencies were also published by the United Nations, the thirty-three volumes constituting a complete compendium of international atomic science.

Meanwhile, in response to widespread alarm over the dangers of atomic fallout, the Scientific Committee on the Effects of Atomic Radiation was set up to coordinate information obtainable from member countries and from FAO, WHO, UNESCO, and other organizations. Even if a nuclear war can be avoided there will still be a serious question about the disposal of radioactive wastes from atomic power plants. There is some hope of developing new forms of atomic power that will not produce poisonous ashes, particularly if hydrogen power can be harnessed, but for the time being the dangers are a matter for anxious discussion in the United Nations.

The Committee reported to the General Assembly in 1958, reviewing the existing knowledge of the subject. It concluded that all atomic radiation is a menace to health and to heredity. The less there is of it the fewer people will be struck, but there is no harmless level of pollution with radioactive materials. The Assembly asked the Committee to continue studying the situation and to report every year.

The separation of peaceful atomic developments from the weapons problem is designed to contribute to the pressures for a peaceful solution. That is why the proponents of Atoms for Peace refused to accept the proposal to connect it with the discussion of atomic disarmament. As Henry Cabot Lodge, the United States delegate, said on November 15, 1954:

Disarmament is one element in the building of peace. At least one other element is a new world outlook which may get us into the habit of working together and thus, eventually, of trusting each other. We think that this "Atoms for Peace" proposal will lead the world away from war because it is a new prism through which we can look at the problems of the world. It is a new place at which to begin.

In November, 1959, the Director-General of IAEA told the General Assembly that the Agency was beginning to show results. About six hundred students from forty-two countries had already been selected for advanced training and some fifty experts had been engaged to help countries in planning for the use of atomic power. A research laboratory was under construction in Vienna, and several dozen research contracts had been let to existing laboratories. The program for supplying uranium to member states was not as far advanced, but one sale of three tons of natural uranium had been made to Japan for use in a research reactor.

The Director-General pointed out that actual use of atomic power plants was delayed by their high cost as compared with ordinary coal or oil burning plants, together with the recent appearance of surplus quantities of these fuels in the markets. Atomic power was something for the future in countries where coal or oil are still plentiful, though it might soon be worth using where the old-fashioned fuels are scarce and expensive. Accordingly, the chief immediate activities of IAEA must be in training, research, and planning.

Aside from atomic power, the Agency studies the rapidly growing field of application of radioactive materials in medicine, industry, and agriculture, the protection of workers and the public from harmful radiation, the safe disposal of waste materials, and the safeguards against illegitimate use.

In the debate following the 1959 report, the Communist states complained that too much attention was being given to safeguards and inspection, even to the extent of using this feature as an excuse for interference with the domestic affairs of some of the member countries. They also objected to IAEA technical assistance to Chiang Kai-shek; to which the Chinese representative replied that his Government was one of the founders of IAEA, and that it was regrettable that the atmosphere of hope and harmony should be marred by the Soviet Union and its satellites.

But in the main all the members felt that the work of the IAEA was of increasing value to the future prosperity of the world, and that in the long run it would be an instrument for the kind of cooperation that points the way to peace.

THE ORGANIZATION
OF THE UNITED NATIONS

When the League of Nations was founded in 1919, it had an important new feature. The League was designed to be a continuing organization of the nations for peace and progress along every line of action. There had been international organizations for limited purposes, such as the Universal Postal Union. There had been great peace conferences and disarmament conferences, but they met, discussed, passed resolutions, and dissolved. The League was intended to be permanent, carrying on a growing body of tradition that the members would come to treat with respect. The League was destroyed in World War II, but the idea had taken root.

In particular, the people of the United States, more than half of whom had wanted to join the League in 1920, were determined in 1945 to join a new United Nations Organization.

The nations that met at San Francisco early in 1945 came with the purpose of setting up a permanent world organization with a more complete program of work than the League had had. None of them wanted to create a world government, however. For that reason it is not realistic to judge the United Nations by the standards used in classifying governments, such as, for instance, democratic representation, law enforcement, or the taxing power. Instead of hunting for traces of government, it is better to take the organization as it is and see what it is supposed to do, and how it is equipped to do it.

The General Assembly

The General Assembly is the central, or principal, organ of the UN, and is made up of all the member nations.

Each member can send five representatives to the Assembly, but in any case each member has only one vote.

The General Assembly elects its own President and Vice-Presidents for each session. While the Secretary-General is the chief UN official, the President of the Assembly is the most prominent individual in the United Nations while the Assembly is in session. Both these officials have so far been chosen with great care and success and have exerted a powerful influence for the advancement of the UN, an influence based not only on their positions but on their own characters.

The Assembly appoints committees of many kinds to prepare the work for its regular sessions.

The seven Main Committees discuss items on the agenda and recommend action. Every member nation can have a representative on each of these Committees.

There are smaller committees on credentials, budget, and other "housekeeping" details. There are also special committees to deal with problems such as Korean reunification, the care of refugees, the effects of atomic radiaction, or the peaceful uses of outer space.

The Assembly adopts the general budget of the UN and assesses the members for their shares of the budget according to their ability to pay. Such factors as national income, average income per person, temporary dislocation of national income, and ability to obtain foreign money, are taken into consideration. The UN budget for 1959 was about $60,000,000, and the assessments ranged from 33.3 per cent of the total for the United States and 13.96 per cent for the Soviet Union down to 0.04 per cent for several of the small countries such as Haiti and Iceland. The fact that every member has to pay what the Assembly demands or resign does not make the Assembly a government. The same power is found in any private club.

The General Assembly may consider any question related to peace and security and to the promotion of world prosperity and justice, except matters that are being acted upon by the Security Council, and matters that are strictly the internal affairs of member nations. In practice, if the Security Council votes and action is blocked by a veto, the question is then open for the Assembly to take it up. As for the definition of "internal affairs," there have been many disputes. Powers that hold colonies, for instance, often take the position that the affairs of the colonies are internal and not open to UN discussion. The smaller nations, especially those recently freed from colonial status, want to discuss the complaints of dependent territories. The tendency is for the UN to take more and more interest in the dependent areas.

All UN agencies report directly or indirectly to the General Assembly, and it may discuss their activities and recommend changes. The Assembly decides important questions—including those on UN organizational matters such as the election of members to the UN or to the Security Council and Trusteeship Council—by a two-thirds vote. All other matters are decided by a simple majority.

The Security Council

The Security Council is made up of eleven members. Five of these are permanent members, being the five Great Powers as of 1945—China, France, the United Kingdom, the United States, and the U.S.S.R. The other six are elected by the General Assembly for two-year terms, three each year.

The original intention was that the Security Council should have a military force at its command, which it could use to keep order among the nations. In signing the Charter, the members agreed to obey the decisions of the Council, which therefore has in theory certain legislative powers within the field of its job as policeman.

In practice, however, the Council has not been able to agree on how to organize a UN police force. Moreover, except in the case of Korea, it has not been able to agree on the use of force. Its legislative powers therefore have almost dried up. In their place, the Assembly has enlarged its ability to make recommendations, backed only by moral force, which appears to be more potent than UN police power.

The Security Council requires a vote of any seven out of the eleven members to pass a decision on what is called a "procedural" matter—any internal question not directly affecting outside interests. "Substantive" matters require a vote of seven, including all five permanent members. This is the so-called "veto" of the five Great Powers. If a member is a party to a dispute, however, it must abstain from voting; in practice, an abstention by a permanent member is not regarded as a veto.

Any nation, whether a member of the UN or not, may bring to the attention of the General Assembly or the Security Council any dispute that seems likely to lead to a breach of the peace. Both bodies have wide powers under the Charter to attempt peaceful methods of settlement before using force or the recommendation of force.

The Council has a right of veto on the admission of new members to the UN, which it has often used.

The Economic and Social Council (ECOSOC)

ECOSOC is made up of eighteen member states, elected by the General Assembly for three-year terms in groups of six each year. This is the general committee of the Assembly to promote higher standards of living, better health, respect for human rights, and international cooperation in education and the arts.

ECOSOC has created many commissions and committees to study and report on various subjects ranging from the economic condition of Europe to the international opium trade. It is the UN body that makes agreements with the specialized agencies, such as the Food and Agriculture Organization (FAO) or the Universal Postal Union (UPU), subject to the approval of the General Assembly.

ECOSOC is also authorized to recognize nongovernmental organizations having technical knowledge that may help it in its work. More than thirteen hundred such organizations have been given what is called "consultative status." They are permitted to send observers to public meetings of the Council and its commissions. They may also speak at such meetings and present written statements which will be circulated as documents of these bodies.

The consulting organizations include, for example, the International Chamber of Commerce, International Confederation of Free Trade Unions, International Association of Juvenile Court Judges, Rotary International, Salvation Army, and International Islamic Economic Organization.

ECOSOC reports regularly to the General Assembly and often brings forward questions upon which the Assembly may wish to pass resolutions.

The other main UN organs are the Trusteeship Council,

described in Chapter 6, and the International Court of Justice, described in Chapter 7.

The Secretary-General

The Secretary-General is the chief administrative officer of the United Nations, and he also has important political responsibilities.

The Secretary-General is "appointed by the General Assembly upon the recommendation of the Security Council." This means that before being voted upon by the General Assembly, the name of a proposed Secretary-General must be approved by the Council subject to the veto of any one of the five permanent members. This requirement enhances the importance of the Secretary-General, for he has been accepted by all the Great Powers, at least at the time of his election. He is therefore in a position to stand above the conflict and to mediate in times of severe tension.

The Charter gives the Secretary-General the privilege of coming before the Security Council to present for its consideration any matter that in his opinion may threaten the peace. The first Secretary-General, Trygve Lie, developed this privilege to include direct mediation among delegates to bring reconciliation of conflicts, when no other person was in a position to take the initiative. As his successor said in 1957: "I believe . . . that the Secretary-General should . . . help in filling any vacuum that may appear in the systems which the Charter and traditional diplomacy provide for the safeguarding of peace and security."

Trygve Lie of Norway, the first Secretary-General, was appointed on February 1, 1946 for five years. In 1950, when the Security Council was unable to agree on a recommendation regarding his successor, he was continued in office for a further three years. After two years, however, he resigned and Dag Hammarskjold of Sweden was appointed for a term of five years. Mr. Hammarskjold was sworn into office on April 10, 1953. In September 1957 he was reappointed for a further five-year term.

Every year the Secretary-General makes a report to the General Assembly on the work of the Organization. He also acts as administrative officer for the meetings of the Assembly, the Security Council, the Trusteeship Council, and ECOSOC. In these jobs he employs various members of the Secretariat, of which he is the executive head.

The Secretariat

In the UN headquarters in New York is a staff of over three thousand people working directly under the Secretary-General. There are other headquarters, in Geneva, Bangkok, The Hague, Montreal, Santiago de Chile, and so on, where specialized agencies or branches of the UN have other hundreds of employees.

There is no place in the world where people from so many different nations work in the same organization as at the UN in New York. UN employees come to the Secretariat from nearly every country on earth, including some countries that do not belong to the UN. But they do not represent their countries. According to Article 100 of the Charter, the Secretary-General and the staff shall not seek or receive instructions from any other authority external to the Organization. Moreover, each member undertakes not to seek to influence its own nationals who are on the staff.

The delegates to the Assembly represent their countries and get instructions from home; their countrymen on the staff do not.

How about the betrayal of secrets? There are no secrets that involve the security of a country. Tourists are not allowed loose in the Secretariat office building because they would interfere with the work; but the information in the building is open to delegates from all countries.

The UN buildings contain nearly all the equipment and services that the Organization needs. There is even a fire department to take care of small fires, though in case of a serious fire the New York City Fire Department would come to help. There are restaurants, a bank, a library, and a post office, though the delegates and staff have to find lodgings outside.

There is an international school in Manhattan for the children of UN delegates and staff. In May of 1960 it had about 330 children from 47 countries, and 34 teachers from 14 different countries, most of them speaking two or more languages.

The UN post office is operated by the United States Post

Office, but the UN Postal Administration, a part of the Secretariat, issues its own stamps, valid on mail posted at Headquarters to any part of the world.

The staff has an elaborate job to do in managing the meetings in the New York Headquarters. The topics to be discussed must be examined and the necessary background material made ready for delegates to use when they need it. All the necessary interpreters have to be on hand to translate all the languages that the delegates at any meeting will speak. Stenographers record the proceedings in English, French, Spanish, Chinese, and Russian. The speeches are also piped to a recording room where they are permanently recorded.

The "simultaneous interpreters" sit in soundproof booths overlooking the meeting, listening to the speaker and translating at the same time. Thus the dials at every seat can be turned to give the proceedings in English, French, Spanish, Chinese, or Russian by setting the dial. In the meetings of the Security Council and the Disarmament Commission two "consecutive interpreters" also listen to the speaker. When he has finished they repeat the whole speech, with appropriate emphasis and gestures. in English and in French, if he has spoken in any other language.

The United Nations *Journal* prints summaries of the day's meetings in English and French. It is printed during the night to be available the next day.

The Department of Public Information publishes books, pamphlets, and magazines describing the work of the UN; it directs the Headquarters bookstore, and has sales outlets all over the world. It has shown documentary films in over ninety countries. with sound tracks in more than thirty languages. The DPI issues press releases, but these are not exclusive; it gives every facility to newsmen to write their own dispatches from "United Nations, N.Y."

Radio news broadcasts by the UN staff go out in some thirty languages for all regions of the world, telling what happened during the day. The UN reporters do not "slant" the news to favor any side of an argument, so their reports are well received all over the world.

The records of the UN proceedings are preserved in a file room with special protection against fire. There are also more than three thousand treaties contained in safes, for under the Charter all treaties must be registered with the

UN and published by it. If a treaty is not registered, no UN organ will recognize it as binding.

The UN Headquarters staff does a considerable amount of scientific and statistical work that is not covered by any of the agency staffs in other parts of the world. The New York staff has made studies, for instance, of the rights of women, the newest methods of house construction, the growth of national populations, and a proposal for a set of standard road signs that can be understood without words. The staff collects information for all the UN organs and agencies. It also handles the expenses and draws up the budget for the Secretary-General to present to the Assembly.

About a million tourists visit the New York Headquarters every year. Guides are provided to show groups of tourists around. You can be admitted to the galleries of the meeting halls as long as there are vacant seats.

The guards will not allow you to make a speech from the galleries. They do not have the right to arrest people but they can put disorderly tourists out into New York, U.S.A.

Costs of the UN

The UN, being an organization that deals mainly in moral force and the exchange of knowledge, costs almost nothing in comparison with international enterprises that have to meet material needs. For the regular UN budget of about $60,000,000, the United States contributes the equivalent of about 10 cents per head of its population; some other nations, with smaller contributions, pay more per head.

For comparison, the original Marshall Plan was estimated to cost $24 billion, or six hundred times the UN yearly budget. Of the various special programs, in 1959, UNICEF used nearly $27,000,000, UNRWA $38,000,000 for care of Arab refugees, and the Expanded Program of Technical Assistance over $31,000,000.

These funds are raised by special contributions from governments and private givers, and are not paid directly by the UN. All the specialized agencies have their own membership, which may differ from that of the UN, and assess their own dues, getting no subsidies from other UN funds except the Technical Assistance Fund and the Special Fund.

The UN activities that are agreed by the members to be essential for protecting and building the peace are rapidly rising in cost, and the small budgets of the Organization and its affiliated agencies need to be considerably increased. The amounts needed are small compared with the national budgets of the members, but there are always political obstacles to such appropriations, which can be overcome only by wide and hearty public support.

The biggest costs of international action are, of course, the costs of armament. They are coordinated by the regional organizations and paid for by the nations outside the UN budget. In this setting it is evident that if the UN could profitably use twice as much money, the members could afford to supply it with no noticeable effect on their finances.

Amending the Charter

The Charter provided that the Assembly and Security Council must consider in 1955 whether to hold a special Convention for amending the Charter. This is one of the two ways in which amendments can be submitted to the members. The other is for the Assembly to approve an Amendment by a vote of two-thirds of the membership.

But in any case a proposed amendment must go to the members for ratification and cannot come into force until it is ratified by two-thirds of the members including the Big Five. That is, the veto may stand in the way of final ratification.

But the Charter, though hard to amend by formal voting, is flexible, like the Constitution of the United States. Just as the people of the United States have quietly mummified the Electoral College and have built up the political parties, not mentioned in the Constitution, so the UN, finding the Security Council often unable to act, has been shifting its duties to other organs not paralyzed by any veto power.

The most important informal changes from the original UN, as conceived at San Francisco, include the following:

The UN armed forces, provided in Article 43, have practically been dropped. (The UNEF used in Egypt is quite a different thing.) Articles 44 to 48, giving details of how the UN forces shall be used, are dead, at least for the present. Article 106, authorizing the Big Five to act as a temporary Security Council, never has come alive because of the quick-growing disagreements among the Big Five. Article 23 provides that the Assembly shall elect the temporary members of the Security Council with due regard to their contributions to peace. This requirement turned out not to be practical.

On the positive side, several additions have been made to the original Charter. One was the agreement in the Security Council that when a permanent member fails to vote, that is not a veto. The Assembly has repeatedly pressed the Council to classify more topics as not subject to veto.

The increased influence of the Secretary-General has made this office more important than as originally conceived. Another change is the Assembly's insistence on discussing the treatment of dependent territories, a subject not positively allowed by the language of the Charter except in the Trusteeships.

The Uniting for Peace resolutions drastically changed the relationships originally intended to be established by the Charter between the Security Council and the Assembly.

Another example of how the UN is able to meet an unforeseen responsibility is the way it took over the problem of the Italian colonies. It was strictly the right of the conquering powers—Britain, France, the United States, and the U.S.S.R.—to settle the future of Libya, Somaliland, and Eritrea. After three years of negotiating and inability to agree, the four Powers agreed to let the Assembly decide. There have been clear signs of a demand that the UN take sovereignty over various wild areas, including the sea bottom, the South Polar Continent, and outer space. In general, however, the Assembly may only make recommendations, and the nations concerned will afterwards decide whether to accept them or not.

A number of supplementary agreements among various member states have spelled out some details not covered in the Charter but consistent with it. One is the treaty with the United States defining the legal position of the Headquarters district in New York. Most important are the regional treaties supplementing UN efforts to keep the peace, such as the North Atlantic Treaty and the Organiza-

tion of American States. There is also a Convention on
Privileges and Immunities, defining the rights of UN
officials, property, funds, and communications.

There is within the UN a strong resistance to formal
amendment of the Charter, and since 1955 the calling of a
special convention has been repeatedly postponed. At the
same time, the Organization is able to change its ways of
operating to meet unforeseen dangers and problems.

THE PHILOSOPHY
OF THE UNITED NATIONS

The Rockefeller Panel Report on U.S. Foreign Policy, in 1959, declared:
"The UN stands, finally, as a symbol of the world order that will be built. . . . To measure the UN's contribution, one need only ask how much meaner and poorer, how much less touched by hope or reason, would be the world scene if it suddenly ceased to exist."

When the victorious nations met at San Francisco in 1945 to organize for peace there was one choice that had already been made—they had chosen to set up a world-wide organization, a new and better organized League of Nations. Everyone knew that there were serious differences among the nations on various questions. If the nations were going to set up a world-wide organization, its charter would have to be loose enough to tolerate nations with deeply antagonistic views. On the other hand, if they had intended to found a true federal government with full power to enforce its laws against any rebellious state, then the UN would have to be composed entirely of nations that were agreed on the most controversial issues. In other words, the UN could have had a stronger charter, if only one class of nations, such as the "Western world," or the Americas, had been in it. Such a like-minded combination might have been able to do without the veto, as the Organization of American States has done. But it would not have been any kind of a world organization.

The decision to hold the San Francisco meeting was a decision to create a world organization that would include all the hostile camps that might be destined to take form. However much division might come into the world—over communism, or colonialism, or race and religious conflicts, or the difference between rich and poor countries—so long as the UN goes on there would be a place where the contending parties could argue in the presence of others who are more concerned for peace then they are for the victory of either side. Such a relationship might not prevent the fatal World War III, but in the opinion of the statesmen of all parties, such an organized arguing place is the best hope of preventing it.

With that belief in the desperate necessity of having a world-wide United Nations, the delegates at San Francisco created "as strong an organization as all of them could agree upon and as, in their judgment, could, in practice, be effective at this stage in the history of the world." These are the words of Trygve Lie, the first Secretary-General of the UN.

The Charter binds all the members, including the Great Powers, to work for peace and not to use or threaten force on their own account against any nation. It binds the members to help the UN in suppressing aggression and to give no help to the aggressors. If all the Great Powers would faithfully keep these promises there would be no world war, even if some small nation might occassionally have to be reduced to order. But if one of the Great Powers should break the peace and if the other should decide to resist by force, no possible world organization could suppress the Powers on either side of such a conflict.

What a world organization can do, and what it is doing fairly well, is to lead the Great Powers to look before they leap. If the small nations do not like what the Powers are doing, they can say so and the Powers feel called upon to answer. While they argue, it is possible that crisis after crisis can come and go without quite heating up to the explosion point. If the UN is to act as a forum for arguing among hostile nations, it cannot use force against any nation that is big enough to blow up the forum itself. This is the reason that the United States insisted on the "veto," and the other Great Powers joined in demanding it as a condition of signing the Charter.

The Veto

The veto embodied in the Charter prevents the Security Council from using force against anyone except by a vote of seven out of the eleven members, including the "concurring votes" of all of the five permanent members.

The veto is a recognition of the fact that the limit of the UN's power to use its own police force is a limit short of world war. If the disagreements among the Great Powers should ever reach the point where one of these Powers must be disciplined by military action, the UN would no longer be in the picture, and the fatal third war would already be beyond hope of remedy. The veto is a safeguard against fatally big ideas in the UN itself—big ideas of enforcing peace in a situation where no human agency could enforce it. The UN is warned that its job of keeping the peace does not include any kind of disciplinary action that would bring on the world war.

The police powers of the Security Council, therefore, cannot be used in such a way as to corner one of the Great Powers and force it to fight. The veto is a built-in protection against UN action that would surely start a new world war.

Experience has shown that the Assembly, in which there is no veto, can "act" in cases where the Security Council must not "act," simply because the Assembly's action is purely moral and advisory. World opinion is a strong force, but it does not kill soldiers or civilians, and therefore does not have to be answered by a shooting war.

It is true that in several ways the UN as a peacemaker has not worked out as the San Francisco Conference expected. On the minus side there were two serious disappointments: the failure to settle World War II; and the excessive use of the veto.

Remains of World War II

One disappointment is that the peace treaties to end World War II did not come through quickly. It was expected that the victorious Powers would impose peace on the defeated Axis and the UN could start from there. But as it has worked out, the Powers have not been able to agree on peace terms for the principal Axis countries. Treaties were signed only with the East European allies of Germany that came under Soviet control, and these treaties have been a continual bone of contention between the Western Powers and the Soviet Union.

The years went by and the Powers could not agree on

treaties for Japan or Germany. In Japan there were no Soviet troops, and so the Western Powers could make their own peace with that country, leaving it still at war with the U.S.S.R. (Later the Soviet Union also made peace with Japan and that country was admitted to the UN.) In Germany part of the country is under Soviet control, and that control cannot be lifted except by a peace in which the Soviet Government will join. The Western Powers have made as much peace as they can with the part of Germany not controlled by the Soviets. The Germans find it a poor substitute for freedom and reunion.

These stubborn remains of World War II create problems that threaten world peace—problems such as the Berlin blockade and the disputes about how to unify Germany. These problems concern the UN, although in theory it was not intended that the UN should take an interest in the defeated countries until peace had been signed. The UN Assembly does not hesitate to urge the Powers to hasten the final peace treaties. In time its constant moral pressure may be the force that overcomes the last obstacles to the final ending of the war.

Too Many Vetoes

The second disappointment in the peace machinery has been the frequent use of the veto by the Soviet representative in the Security Council. At San Francisco, the Great Powers all agreed in insisting on the right of veto. None of them wanted to be committed without its own consent to fighting a war even to enforce peace. They went further. They also agreed that the right of veto in the Council should apply to everything except procedural questions. The theory advanced by the Great Powers in support of such sweeping rights of veto was that once the Security Council takes jurisdiction over any international dispute, even in an effort to reach a peaceful settlement, a chain of events is set in motion that may end with military enforcement action. They made one exception. This was the proviso that if one of them were a party to a dispute, it must abstain from voting while the Council tries to reach a peaceful settlement.

The veto in this form was accepted with a good deal of reluctance by the smaller countries. Unfortunately there are many cases where the veto can be used that do not fit the arguments for it that were advanced at San Francisco. For example, most of the vetoes cast by the Soviet Union have been against the admission of various countries to membership in the United Nations. In some other decisions, the Soviet delegate has voted "No" to a proposal that happened not to conform to the Soviet line of policy.

On the other hand, the Soviet veto of various disarmament proposals, although it has been distressing to the other members, is not necessarily an abuse of the veto power. Any disarmament treaty, to be effective, must be willingly and loyally accepted by all the Great Powers. If the terms of a proposed treaty are not acceptable to any Power, it can of course prevent that treaty by merely refusing to sign. The veto, therefore, is no more than notification of the plain fact that the proposals are not unanimously accepted. This may be an unpleasant fact, but the veto is not what makes it so.

In the Assembly the smaller nations, who naturally resent the veto power, have a majority of the votes, and the Assembly has voted from time to time to admonish the Powers about their use of the veto. It is hard to see how anything more effective for changing the use of the veto could be found. There is no force on earth capable of making a Power give up what it regards as its legal rights, unless it may be the force of world opinion.

There are, of course, many people who would like to see the Charter amended so as to restrict or abolish the veto power. The Charter cannot be amended according to its own terms except with the concurrence of the Big Five —that is, any amendment can be vetoed. This also has reason, for if the smaller nations could unite to change the Charter over the objections of any Great Power, that Power would be likely to resign, and for practical purposes there would be no United Nations. Here, also, the veto represents the unpleasant difference between the real world and a much more orderly but imaginary one.

Propaganda

Once the fundamental decision was taken to set up a world-wide organization, another unpleasant consequence necessarily followed. In the UN there has to be free speech. Everyone who belongs has a right to say whatever he wants to say, right or wrong, honest or dishonest. That is, the UN can be used by adversaries as a platform for their propaganda. Their opponents sometimes feel that if only they could be thrown out how it would clear the air! No more big lies, no more campaigns of hate and vilification. Peace and quiet would settle over the Council and the Assembly. But it would be the same kind of peace and quiet that we find in the inner councils of a nation at war, where the enemies are outside and only friends are inside.

It is not a black mark against the United Nations that in its halls the most flimsy arguments and the most subtle deceptions can be laid before the meeting and solemnly put into the official record. This is one of the principal advantages of the UN. If there is any nation in the world that is putting out dishonest propaganda, the place where that propaganda is most likely to be poisonous is in private arguments, among ignorant or ill-balanced people. It has little chance of deceiving UN delegates, who have heard all sides many times over.

On the contrary, in the UN, if there is any dishonest propaganda afloat, the author of it must bring it in under the withering inspection of men of all nations and religions, including his own allies. Or if he tries to hide anything, his opponents will drag it in. The fearful heat of world moral judgment is proved by the desperate efforts of those who are in the wrong to defend themselves by arguments which they hope will cover them.

No Great Power would dare to state its sovereign will in the United Nations Assembly and then sit tight and wait for the lesser nations to cringe before it. No matter how arrogant a Power may be in its actions, it has to talk. The smaller nations do not cringe. They rise and say what they think.

So long as men can do wrong and tell lies, one of the greatest values of a market place of opinion is that such men are on view in the market. In the long run, open disagreements openly arrived at are more likely to be settled according to the moral judgment of mankind than secret plottings covered by a veil of silence.

World Government?

The question is often raised whether the UN is a sort of baby world government that in time will grow up to rule the nations with a world system of law, a world police, and a world income tax. Those who are impatient to see a world government criticize the UN for failing to be one or to show signs of growing into one.

Those who fear the thought of a world government criticize the UN for being the entering camel's head in the door of the tent that in time will be followed by the whole beast.

Any positive statement on this question has to be hedged around with qualifications because the meanings of the necessary words can be easily misinterpreted. What, for instance, is a government? If you consider a city government, a provincial or state government, and a national government, they are plainly not the same thing, especially in their relation to that final authority called "sovereignty." In the United States, for instance, the final authority to use force against the citizen—that is, the police power—rests in some cases with the state and in others with the federal government. It is not a simple matter to picture what a world government would be like if there were to be one.

Another fact that needs to be considered is that in the long run all governments that are freely set up by the people "depend on the consent of the governed." The UN was not designed to pave the way for any dictator to conquer the world. If any world government should grow up under the benevolent auspices of the UN, it would depend on the consent of the people of the world. So far as anyone can see now, the people of the world are not prepared to give the UN or any other authority enough powers to add up to a recognizable federal government of the world.

During the Suez and Hungarian crises of 1956–57 there was some criticism of the UN on the ground that it had a "double standard" of judgment, since it procured the withdrawal of the Israeli, French, and British troops from Egypt but did not get the Soviet troops out of Hungary. This criticism may have been based upon an unspoken and perhaps unconscious assumption that the UN ought to act like a world government—judging the nations under world law and forcing them to obey the law. That is not what the UN is for, and the people of the world have given it no such authority.

The UN applied a single standard of moral judgment in its requests and recommendations on the Suez situation and on Hungary. It expressed the moral judgment of the majority of the nations, but it had not been given the legal

right or the power to force anyone to obey. The Soviet
Government refused to comply with the UN requests, and
the only penalty was the condemnation expressed in the
Report on Hungary as accepted by the Assembly.

The fact that the UN is not authorized to make war on
the Soviet Union in Hungary's behalf reflects, as the
Secretary-General declared in his annual report, "the pro-
found will of the peoples of the world to avoid general
war." It is much easier for private persons to call for
"enforcement" of what they are sure is right than for the
responsible leaders of the nations to find a path through
the minefields of the world with some hope of avoiding
total disaster.

The peoples of the world are not prepared to give any
central world authority the final sovereign powers that
characterize a federal nation like the United States—such
as the final power to tax the citizen, to punish citizens for
crimes, to draft them for the World Army, and to control
the rules of trade regardless of the desires of the nations.
In general, they are not ready to let any central legislature
make international law without the consent of the nations.

If the world's peoples should ever be ready for such a
federal government, it would be when they have decided
that the conflicts among peoples, classes, races, and religions are no harder to compromise than they are in a
federal government such as the United States. That will
be a long time, if ever.

But there are some parts of the relations among sovereign states that can be administered by a world authority
with the consent of each nation that accepts the authority.
For instance, everyone recognizes that the mails must be
carried between countries under rules established for the
world. The Universal Postal Union was the first world
authority to be set up, and all civilized nations have to
belong to it. Equally good reasons have led to the creation
of the other specialized agencies governing the relations of
their members along certain lines of action.

These organizations are voluntary arrangements, and
are not imposed on unwilling countries by any supergov-
ernment. The nations organize certain activities in order
to prevent confusion and prohibitive costs of doing business. The specialized agencies are useful in themselves
and they also are useful in bringing even unfriendly nations to sit together for a practical purpose.

The same general principle applies to international law, as it is called. The United Nations cannot pass an international law binding on any nation without its specific assent, except in the rare case where the Security Council, with all the permanent members consenting, can order a pair of smaller nations to stop fighting and start talking. The Assembly can pass a resolution advising the nations what to do, but if the nations refuse, the only punishment is a resolution of the Assembly condemning their refusal. This moral power is a strong power but it is not law.

The UN can cause international law to be created by the free consent of the nations in at least two ways.

The Conventions that the UN offers to the nations become international law for all the nations that ratify them. A treaty is a piece of international law, enforced not by any international police but by the moral penalties of dishonor that fall on treaty-breakers. The day of 100 per cent obedience to international law by all the nations may be as far off as the day when all men honor their personal promises, but there is nevertheless a moral penalty for broken faith that is not to be despised.

In another way the United Nations can be said to sponsor the making of law. In the International Court of Justice, those nations that voluntarily submit themselves to the Court can be judged like the citizens of any sovereign state. If a nation is accused by another nation or by the UN of violating its treaty obligations, the Court may judge not only the facts but the interpretation of the treaty, and its interpretation will then be the law.

Is this then the subtle beginning of a world government that will take away the sovereignty of the free nations? The question sounds ominous, but in fact it has no immediate meaning. What instruments of agreement the nations freely decide to adopt among themselves are surely within the sovereign power of each nation that chooses to join. The moral obligation to honor promises freely made is no tyranny. If the obligation of honor is imposed by any Power higher than the nations, that Authority is not one that God-fearing men dare resent. And back of that moral Authority is the hard fact that peaceful agreement and cooperation are the way of life, in a world where the Last Judgment is more than likely to happen soon, and a way of life is desperately wanted.

Who Can Belong?

The question of admitting new members to the United Nations is not so much a legal matter of interpretation of the Charter as a question of what sort of institution the United Nations is intended to be.

When the Charter was written in 1945, the obligation of the members to work sincerely for peace was emphasized. Surely all peoples want peace, and all nations worthy of membership in the new league for peace must be peace-loving. The defeated Axis Powers, of course, were to be suitably re-educated and purified, until they too became peace-loving and fit to join with the decent nations. Everyone knew there would be quarrels, but it seemed reasonable to say in Article 4 of the Charter that membership is open to all other "peace-loving" states if they accept the obligations of the Charter and in the judgment of the Organization are able and willing to carry out these obligations.

Before the Charter was signed a question arose about the Ukraine and Byelorussia, which to the rest of the world appeared to be not free states able to accept any obligations to the UN but mere provinces of the Soviet Union subject to the federal government in Moscow. To the Soviet delegates, on the other hand, it seemed plain enough that Canada, Australia, and the other Dominions would be under the orders of the British Government, and that all the Latin American states were mere satellites of the United States that would have to vote as ordered by Washington. These suppositions may not have all been true, but they had to be taken into account, and so the original members included some that in the judgment of most of the Organization were hardly "able and willing" to carry out the obligations of free Charter members.

During the first ten years, however, only nine additional countries were added to the original fifty-one Charter members. No state can be admitted without the "recommendation" of the Security Council. The Soviet delegate vetoed all applicants that were in any way objectionable to his country, such as the Republic of Korea, Libya, Italy, and Japan. The majority of the Council turned down all those that it regarded as under Soviet control, such as Hungary, Romania, and Bulgaria.

171

In 1946 the United States suggested a compromise by which the candidates of both factions would be admitted, but the Soviets refused. Later the Soviets wanted a "package deal," and the Western nations refused. Finally in 1955 it was arranged, and sixteen nations were admitted at one time. Later additions brought the total membership to eighty-two in 1960. Still excluded by Soviet objections were South Vietnam and the ROK, and by Western objections North Vietnam, North Korea, and Outer Mongolia.

There is wide agreement that in the long run the UN ought to include all the independent nations of the world. But how many shortcomings to overlook for the sake of universal membership will long be a matter of dispute. In view of the fact that most nations have some faults in their UN behavior, and that no nation however proudly sovereign is absolutely independent, the arguments are bound to contain much cloudy judgment about where to draw the line. There is, however, no doubt that the central philosophy of the UN, accepted by all the members, includes the belief that some day its membership should include every nation on earth.

One Member, One Vote

The General Assembly of the United Nations, where every member state has one vote, is analogous to the Senate of the United States, in which the states, large and small, have an equal voice. Is this democratic?

The democracy of the United Nations, like that of the United States, is affected by the peculiarity of having to take account of the rights of large and small states as well as the rights of people. The UN is in the main a democracy of nations, not of individual human beings. In a rough way there is a touch of popular democracy in the Security Council, where the veto gives the biggest nations—at least in a military sense as of 1945—a bigger voice than the smaller ones. There have been proposals that the Charter should be amended to "weight" the votes of the members in the Assembly according to their population, but it is not clear how to draw an acceptable amendment.

In the Assembly, where most of the vitality of the UN has become concentrated, Costa Rica and Lebanon have as many votes as the United Kingdom and the United States. This is not democratic in the sense of giving every human being equal voting weight in the Assembly.

If the Assembly were a legislature with power to make laws binding on the nations, the strong would of course not consent to be members, any more than the big states of the United States would consent to be governed by the U.S. Senate alone, without the balancing force of the House of Representatives where they are represented in proportion to their population. But the UN General Assembly was not set up to make world law. It is an organ set up to discuss world affairs and express as nearly as possible the moral judgments of the world. Voting is a part of this expression but not the chief part. The moral force in the Assembly, by which it can hurt a nation that is doing wrong and help one that is doing right, depends in the last analysis not on the final vote alone but even more on what was said, who said it, and what the people of the world think of the arguments put forward and of the parts played by'the nations concerned.

Necessarily a strong nation has a greater weight in the arguments than its one vote would seem to indicate, since its actions and intentions are of greater weight in the making of world events. Moreover it is evident that in the UN the members often vote in groups, either following a strong nation that represents the position they favor, or uniting behind some regional or political interest that they have in common. These groupings and evidences of leadership are not invariable except in the Soviet bloc; they normally shift according to the question at issue. In fact, the moral effect of the Assembly's action depends partly on what groupings have been shown in the voting and in the discussion.

With the addition of numerous Asian and African states since 1954, there has been some uneasiness lest an "Afro-Asian bloc" should take to voting against the West, because of resentments brought down from the heyday of colonialism. The record, however, shows no sign of such bloc voting. Apparently, when the Western nations are surely right they will draw strong support in Asia and Africa; on a more doubtful question they will find the vote divided.

It should be clear that there is more in making and applying the judgment of mankind than can be registered by giving either every nation or every individual an equal vote. It may also be worth noting that for the making of peace, the moral position of the small nations is on the face of it better than that of the Great Powers. No one can wreck the world except some Great Power. No little nation, however belligerent, can start a world war if the Great Powers refuse to join. The responsibility for peace therefore rests entirely on the strongest nations, and the pure desire not to be destroyed in other people's quarrels rests in its most undiluted form among the small nations.

It is more than a mere accident that in the United Nations, where men from all sorts of countries meet to discuss human affairs, the small countries so often contribute statesmen of a much greater relative importance than the size of their country. Great men can occur anywhere, in a big or a little country, but they cannot be seen in their full size except on a world stage. The UN provides that stage, and so brings to the help of hard-pressed humanity men who would otherwise have little chance to become known.

The Great Revolutions

The United Nations is not the cause of the great revolutions that are going on at present, though it may well be the ship that will carry the human race alive through the troubled waters. The world is going through at least three different waves of progress at the same time. There have also been waves of backwash toward savagery.

The oldest wave of progress is the anticolonial revolution, now nearing its end. The vast majority of the peoples who came under foreign domination in the four hundred years after the discovery of America are now independent nations, and nearly all the rest are being groomed for independence. The fact that India, Indonesia, and Pakistan are members of the UN does much to give their new governments confidence and dignity, abroad and at home.

The disturbances caused by the anticolonial revolution have not yet calmed down. There are still resentments among those who were recently under foreign rule as well as among the peoples who have not yet become self-governing. These resentments appear in the UN disputes over the treatment of dependent territories.

The next oldest world revolution is the outburst of scientific knowledge and invention that began seriously to transform human society in the Western world during the nineteenth century. This revolution has opened a magical world of rapidly expanding production. There are limits to this expansion but they are not easily understood by millions of hungry people who never before had any hope of escape from lifelong misery. The knowledge of the magic of science has called forth an insistent demand for a share in this magic. The strains that come from impatience cannot be avoided. Impatient people may grasp at false promises and be led into new slavery in search of the bright vision of enough to eat.

The dark sides of the scientific revolution are also to be taken into account. Science has almost no moral principles. It will serve a Hitler almost as well as it will serve a free democracy, enough to create terrible dangers. And science has given us the atom and a hilltop view of the end of the world.

Another ominous aspect of scientific progress is that science will not only serve fairly well an intelligent dictator; it will also undermine any government that is unduly influenced by a selfish and corrupt ruling class. Factories can be built in such a country, and enough progress can be made to stimulate the expectations of the people. But if the government is too weak to collect heavy income taxes and to reform an oppressive landholding system, business and industry cannot prosper. Such countries are frequently in danger of revolution and dictatorship. A dictator can at least promise to "make the trains run on time." But thereafter may follow political tyranny and unrest.

Technical assistance to countries of all sorts will produce results of different kinds. In the long run it is a hard fact that successful use of science to raise the standard of living depends on honest and intelligent management both of industry and of politics. While some nations go on to illustrate this hard fact by racking internal disorders, it is well to have the UN holding up a moral standard for mankind. And that brings us to the third revolution that is sweeping the world.

The third revolution is closely related to the other two. It is the growing demand of oppressed peoples for justice and for democracy in government. In past ages millions of human beings took what came and never dreamed of any escape from whatever masters fate had set over them. That is not so true today. The change from foreign rule to independence has taught men that their foreign masters were not permanent. They think that perhaps their home-grown landlords and money-lenders may also be subject to overthrow. And the coming of the scientific revolution has forced the process of "fundamental education." People who never before knew of any life beyond their village are learning to read and are listening to the radio in the village square. Those who sat in darkness are beginning to see a light, and they will not be quiet. In their own lives are unhappy experiences that they have long resented without hope of escape. Now they have names for wrongs, and angers that call for rights. They want some voice in choosing their governments and in consenting to the laws that will define their rights. This change also disturbs the waters where humanity must navigate.

There are bound to be true prophets and false prophets; true roads toward freedom and false trails leading into slavery. There is progress toward the real future of useful science, political democracy, and decent human relations, and there are misguided doctrines that lead to tyranny and cruelty. All these rolling seas of hope and fear are part of the great discoveries and hopes of humanity. They may be more than all the resources of human wisdom and good will can master. Our race, and with it all living things on earth, may be doomed to die for our failure to control the fearful forces that we have uncovered. But the Atomic Age has gone on year after year without the sound of the last trumpet, while in the committee rooms of the United Nations men struggle and search for the way to chain the deadly forces and stave off the doom. Every year, while the instruments of destruction grow more deadly, the knowledge of the danger and the determination to avoid it take a sterner hold upon all the governments of the world.

If there is any hope of avoiding the end of the world, and if there is any way that the human race can ride out the great revolutions of our days and live, those ways are most likely to be found in the slow, painful, but determined labors of the United Nations of the world.

APPENDIX A

Structure of the United Nations and List of Related Intergovernmental Organizations

1. PRINCIPAL ORGANS OF THE UNITED NATIONS

(A) THE GENERAL ASSEMBLY
Main Committees
First Committee—Political and Security
Special Political Committee (to assist the First Committee)
Second Committee—Economic and Financial
Third Committee—Social, Humanitarian, and Cultural
Fourth Committee—Trusteeship (including Non-Self-Governing Territories)
Fifth Committee—Administrative and Budgetary
Sixth Committee—Legal

Procedural Committees
Credentials Committee
General Committee

Standing Committees
Advisory Committee on Administrative and Budgetary Questions
Committee on Contributions

Subsidiary and Ad Hoc Bodies
Disarmament Commission
UN Scientific Advisory Committee
Scientific Committee on the Effects of Atomic Radiation
Committee on the Peaceful Uses of Outer Space
Peace Observation Commission
Collective Measures Committee
Panel for Inquiry and Conciliation

177

United Nations Relief and Works Agency for Palestine Refugees in the Near East (UNRWA)

UNRWA Advisory Commission

United Nations Conciliation Commission for Palestine

United Nations Commission for the Unification and Rehabilitation of Korea (UNCURK)

United Nations Representative on Hungary

Committee on Arrangements for a Conference for the Purpose of Reviewing the Charter

Interim Committee of the General Assembly

Committee on South-West Africa

Ad Hoc Commission on Prisoners of War

Administrator for Residual Affairs of the UN Korean Reconstruction Agency (UNKRA)

UN Commission to Investigate Conditions for Free Elections in Germany

United Nations Emergency Force (UNEF)

Advisory Committee on UNEF

UN Commission on Permanent Sovereignty over Natural Resources

UN Special Fund

Governing Council of the Special Fund

UN High Commissioner for Refugees

Executive Committee of the Program of the UN High Commissioner for Refugees

Committee on Information from Non-Self-Governing Territories

Special Committee to Study the Principles Which Should Guide Members in Determining Whether or Not an Obligation Exists to Transmit Information Under Article 73 (e)

Subcommittee on the Questionnaire (on Trust Territories)

UN Commissioner for the Supervision of the Plebiscite in the Cameroons under United Kingdom Administration

Board of Auditors

Investments Committee

Negotiating Committee for Extra-Budgetary Funds

UN Administrative Tribunal

Committee on Applications for Review of Administrative Tribunal Judgments

Committee of Experts on the Review of the Activities and Organization of the Secretariat

Committee for the United Nations Memorial Cemetery in Korea

United Nations Staff Pension Committee
Expert Group on the Comprehensive Review of the
    Pension Fund
Consultative Panel on UN Information Policies and
    Program
International Law Commission
Committee Established under General Assembly Resolu-
    tion 1181 (XII)—(Question of Defining Aggres-
    sion.)

(B) THE SECURITY COUNCIL
Military Staff Committee

Standing Committees
Committee of Experts
Committee on the Admission of New Members (to the
    United Nations)

Ad Hoc Bodies
United Nations Commission for Indonesia (adjourned
    sine die)
United Nations Military Observer Group for India and
    Pakistan
United Nations Representative for India and Pakistan
United Nations Truce Supervision Organization in
    Palestine (UNTSO)

(C) ECONOMIC AND SOCIAL COUNCIL
Functional Commissions and Subcommissions
Commission on Human Rights
Subcommission on Prevention of Discrimination and
    Protection of Minorities
Commission on International Commodity Trade
Commission on Narcotic Drugs
Commission on the Status of Women
Population Commission
Special Commission
Statistical Commission

Regional Economic Commissions
Economic Commission for Africa (ECA)
Economic Commission for Asia and the Far East
    (ECAFE)
Economic Commission for Europe (ECE)
Economic Commission for Latin America (ECLA)

Standing Committees
Council Committee on Non-Governmental Organizations
Interim Committee on Program of Conferences
Standing Committee for Industrial Development
Technical Assistance Committee (TAC)

Ad Hoc Committees
Advisory Committee on the Work Program on Industrialization
Committee of Experts for Further Work on the Transport of Dangerous Goods
Committee on Program Appraisals (on economic, social and human rights programs of the UN and related intergovernmental organizations)
Coordination Committee (on coordination among the UN and related intergovernmental organizations)
Economic Committee
Social Committee

Other Bodies reporting to the Council
Drug Supervisory Body (on narcotic drugs)
Permanent Central Opium Board (on narcotic drugs)
United Nations Children's Fund (UNICEF) (established by the General Assembly)
Executive Board of UNICEF

(D) THE TRUSTEESHIP COUNCIL
Standing Committees
Standing Committee on Administrative Unions
Standing Committee on Petitions

Ad Hoc Committees
Ad Hoc Committee on the Basic Questionnaire
Committee on Classification of Communications
Committee on Rural Economic Development of the Trust Territories

(E) THE INTERNATIONAL COURT OF JUSTICE
Chamber of Summary Procedure

(F) THE SECRETARIAT
Offices of the Secretary-General
Executive Office of the Secretary-General
Office of Legal Affairs
Office of the Controller

Office of Personnel
Offices of the Under-Secretaries for Special Political
   Affairs

Other Departments and Offices
Department of Political and Security Council Affairs
Department of Economic and Social Affairs
Department of Trusteeship and Information from Non-
   Self-Governing Territories
Office of Public Information
Office of Conference Services
Office of General Services

II. INTERGOVERNMENTAL ORGANIZATIONS RELATED TO THE UNITED NATIONS

International Atomic Energy Agency (IAEA)
International Labor Organization (ILO)
Food and Agriculture Organization (FAO)
United Nations Educational, Scientific, and Cultural
   Organization (UNESCO)
International Civil Aviation Organization (ICAO)
World Health Organization (WHO)
International Bank for Reconstruction and Development (Bank)
International Finance Corporation (IFC)
International Monetary Fund (Fund)
Universal Postal Union (UPU)
International Telecommunication Union (ITU)
World Meteorological Organization (WMO)
Intergovernmental Maritime Consultative Organization
   (IMCO)

The Contracting Parties to the General Agreement on
Tariffs and Trade (GATT) are affiliated with the UN through
the GATT Secretariat, which was originally established to
serve as the Secretariat for the Interim Commission for the
proposed International Trade Organization (ITO). A permanent Organization for Trade Cooperation (OTC) to administer GATT was projected in a 1955 agreement not yet
in force.

III. INTERAGENCY BODIES

Administrative Committee on Coordination (ACC)
Panel of External Auditors
Technical Assistance Board (TAB)
Consultative Committee on Public Information

Interim Coordinating Committee for International Commodity Arrangements (ICCICA)
    (reports to the United Nations Economic and Social Council)
United Nations Joint Staff Pension Board

APPENDIX B

Charter of the United Nations

SIGNED AT THE UNITED NATIONS CONFERENCE
ON INTERNATIONAL ORGANIZATION,
SAN FRANCISCO, CALIFORNIA, ON JUNE 26, 1945

WE THE PEOPLES OF THE UNITED NATIONS DETERMINED

to save succeeding generations from the scourge of war, which twice in our lifetime has brought untold sorrow to mankind, and

to reaffirm faith in fundamental human rights, in the dignity and worth of the human person, in the equal rights of men and women and of nations large and small, and

to establish conditions under which justice and respect for the obligations arising from treaties and other sources of international law can be maintained, and

to promote social progress and better standards of life in larger freedom,

AND FOR THESE ENDS

to practice tolerance and live together in peace with one another as good neighbors, and

to unite our strength to maintain international peace and security, and

to ensure, by the acceptance of principles and the institution of methods, that armed force shall not be used, save in the common interest, and

to employ international machinery for the promotion of the economic and social advancement of all peoples,

HAVE RESOLVED TO COMBINE OUR EFFORTS
TO ACCOMPLISH THESE AIMS.

Accordingly, our respective Governments, through representatives assembled in the city of San Francisco, who have exhibited their full powers found to be in good and due form, have agreed to the present Charter of the United Nations and do hereby establish an international organization to be known as the United Nations.

CHAPTER I

PURPOSES AND PRINCIPLES

Article 1

The Purposes of the United Nations are:

1. To maintain international peace and security, and to that end: to take effective collective measures for the prevention and removal of threats to the peace, and for the suppression of acts of aggression or other breaches of the peace, and to bring about by peaceful means, and in conformity with the principles of justice and international law, adjustment or settlement of international disputes or situations which might lead to a breach of the peace;

2. To develop friendly relations among nations based on respect for the principle of equal rights and self-determination of peoples, and to take other appropriate measures to strengthen universal peace;

3. To achieve international cooperation in solving international problems of an economic, social, cultural, or humanitarian character, and in promoting and encouraging respect for human rights and for fundamental freedoms for all without distinction as to race, sex, language, or religion; and

4. To be a center for harmonizing the actions of nations in the attainment of these common ends.

Article 2

The Organization and its Members, in pursuit of the Purposes stated in Article 1, shall act in accordance with the following Principles.

1. The Organization is based on the principle of the sovereign equality of all its Members.

2. All Members, in order to ensure to all of them the rights

and benefits resulting from membership, shall fulfil in good faith the obligations assumed by them in accordance with the present Charter.

3. All Members shall settle their international disputes by peaceful means in such a manner that international peace and security, and justice, are not endangered.

4. All Members shall refrain in their international relations from the threat or use of force against the territorial integrity or political independence of any state, or in any other manner inconsistent with the Purposes of the United Nations.

5. All Members shall give the United Nations every assistance in any action it takes in accordance with the present Charter, and shall refrain from giving assistance to any state against which the United Nations is taking preventive or enforcement action.

6. The Organization shall ensure that states which are not Members of the United Nations act in accordance with these Principles so far as may be necessary for the maintenance of international peace and security.

7. Nothing contained in the present Charter shall authorize the United Nations to intervene in matters which are essentially within the domestic jurisdiction of any state or shall require the Members to submit such matters to settlement under the present Charter; but this principle shall not prejudice the application of enforcement measures under Chapter VII.

CHAPTER II

MEMBERSHIP

Article 3

The original Members of the United Nations shall be the states which, having participated in the United Nations Conference on International Organization at San Francisco, or having previously signed the Declaration by United Nations of January 1, 1942, sign the present Charter and ratify it in accordance with Article 110.

Article 4

1. Membership in the United Nations is open to all other peace-loving states which accept the obligations contained in

the present Charter and, in the judgment of the Organization, are able and willing to carry out these obligations.

2. The admission of any such state to membership in the United Nations will be effected by a decision of the General Assembly upon the recommendation of the Security Council.

Article 5

A Member of the United Nations against which preventive or enforcement action has been taken by the Security Council may be suspended from the exercise of the rights and privileges of membership by the General Assembly upon the recommendation of the Security Council. The exercise of these rights and privileges may be restored by the Security Council.

Article 6

A member of the United Nations which has persistently violated the Principles contained in the present Charter may be expelled from the Organization by the General Assembly upon the recommendation of the Security Council.

CHAPTER III

ORGANS

Article 7

1. There are established as the principal organs of the United Nations; a General Assembly, a Security Council, an Economic and Social Council, a Trusteeship Council, an International Court of Justice, and a Secretariat.

2. Such subsidiary organs as may be found necessary may be established in accordance with the present Charter.

Article 8

The United Nations shall place no restrictions on the eligibility of men and women to participate in any capacity and under conditions of equality in its principal and subsidiary organs.

CHAPTER IV

THE GENERAL ASSEMBLY

Composition

Article 9

1. The General Assembly shall consist of all the Members of the United Nations.

2. Each Member shall have not more than five representatives in the General Assembly.

Functions and Powers

Article 10

The General Assembly may discuss any questions or any matters within the scope of the present Charter or relating to the powers and functions of any organs provided for in the present Charter, and, except as provided in Article 12, may make recommendations to the Members of the United Nations or to the Security Council or to both on any such questions or matters.

Article 11

1. The General Assembly may consider the general principles of cooperation in the maintenance of international peace and security, including the principles governing disarmament and the regulation of armaments, and may make recommendations with regard to such principles to the Members or to the Security Council or to both.

2. The General Assembly may discuss any questions relating to the maintenance of international peace and security brought before it by any Member of the United Nations, or by the Security Council, or by a state which is not a Member of the United Nations in accordance with Article 35, paragraph 2, and, except as provided in Article 12, may make recommendations with regard to any such questions to the state or states concerned or to the Security Council or to both. Any such question on which action is necessary shall be referred to the Security Council by the General Assembly either before or after discussion.

3. The General Assembly may call the attention of the Security Council to situations which are likely to endanger international peace and security.

4. The powers of the General Assembly set forth in this Article shall not limit the general scope of Article 10.

Article 12

1. While the Security Council is exercising in respect of

any dispute or situation the functions assigned to it in the present Charter, the General Assembly shall not make any recommendation with regard to that dispute or situation unless the Security Council so requests.

2. The Secretary-General, with the consent of the Security Council, shall notify the General Assembly at each session of any matters relative to the maintenance of international peace and security which are being dealt with by the Security Council and shall similarly notify the General Assembly, or the Members of the United Nations if the General Assembly is not in session, immediately the Security Council ceases to deal with such matters.

Article 13

1. The General Assembly shall initiate studies and make recommendations for the purpose of:

a. promoting international cooperation in the political field and encouraging the progressive development of international law and its codification;

b. promoting international cooperation in the economic, social, cultural, educational, and health fields, and assisting in the realization of human rights and fundamental freedoms for all without distinction as to race, sex, language, or religion.

2. The further responsibilities, functions and powers of the General Assembly with respect to matters mentioned in paragraph 1 (b) above are set forth in Chapter IX and X.

Article 14

Subject to the provisions of Article 12, the General Assembly may recommend measures for the peaceful adjustment of any situation, regardless of origin, which it deems likely to impair the general welfare or friendly relations among nations, including situations resulting from a violation of the provisions of the present Charter setting forth the Purposes and Principles of the United Nations.

Article 15

1. The General Assembly shall receive and consider annual and special reports from the Security Council; these reports shall include an account of the measures that the Security

Council has decided upon or taken to maintain international peace and security.

2. The General Assembly shall receive and consider reports from the other organs of the United Nations.

Article 16

The General Assembly shall perform such functions with respect to the international trusteeship system as are assigned to it under Chapters XII and XIII, including the approval of the trusteeship agreements for areas not designated as strategic.

Article 17

1. The General Assembly shall consider and approve the budget of the Organization.

2. The expenses of the Organization shall be borne by the Members as apportioned by the General Assembly.

3. The General Assembly shall consider and approve any financial and budgetary arrangements with specialized agencies referred to in Article 57 and shall examine the administrative budgets of such specialized agencies with a view to making recommendations to the agencies concerned.

Voting

Article 18

1. Each member of the General Assembly shall have one vote.

2. Decisions of the General Assembly on important questions shall be made by a two-thirds majority of the members present and voting. These questions shall include: recommendations with respect to the maintenance of international peace and security, the election of the non-permanent members of the Security Council, the election of the members of the Economic and Social Council, the election of members of the Trusteeship Council in accordance with paragraph 1 (c) of Article 86, the admission of new Members to the United Nations, the suspension of the rights and privileges of membership, the expulsion of Members, questions relating to the operation of the trusteeship system, and budgetary questions.

3. Decisions on other questions, including the determination of additional categories of questions to be decided by a

two-thirds majority, shall be made by a majority of the members present and voting.

Article 19

A Member of the United Nations which is in arrears in the payment of its financial contributions to the Organization shall have no vote in the General Assembly if the amount of its arrears equals or exceeds the amount of the contributions due from it for the preceding two full years. The General Assembly may, nevertheless, permit such a Member to vote if it is satisfied that the failure to pay is due to conditions beyond the control of the Member.

Procedure

Article 20

The General Assembly shall meet in regular annual sessions and in such special sessions as occasion may require. Special sessions shall be convoked by the Secretary-General at the request of the Security Council or of a majority of the Members of the United Nations.

Article 21

The General Assembly shall adopt its own rules of procedure. It shall elect its President for each session.

Article 22

The General Assembly may establish such subsidiary organs as it deems necessary for the performance of its functions.

CHAPTER V

THE SECURITY COUNCIL

Composition

Article 23

1. The Security Council shall consist of eleven Members of the United Nations. The Republic of China, France, the Union of Soviet Socialist Republics, the United Kingdom of Great Britain and Northern Ireland, and the United States

of America shall be permanent members of the Security Council. The General Assembly shall elect six other Members of the United Nations to be non-permanent members of the Security Council, due regard being specially paid, in the first instance to the contribution of Members of the United Nations to the maintenance of international peace and security and to the other purposes of the Organization, and also to equitable geographical distribution.

2. The non-permanent members of the Security Council shall be elected for a term of two years. In the first election of the non-permanent members, however, three shall be chosen for a term of one year. A retiring member shall not be eligible for immediate re-election.

3. Each member of the Security Council shall have one representative.

Functions and powers

Article 24

1. In order to ensure prompt and effective action by the United Nations, its Members confer on the Security Council primary responsibility for the maintenance of international peace and security, and agree that in carrying out its duties under this responsibility the Security Council acts on their behalf.

2. In discharging these duties the Security Council shall act in accordance with the Purposes and Principles of the United Nations. The specific powers granted to the Security Council for the discharge of these duties are laid down in Chapter VI, VII, VIII, and XII.

3. The Security Council shall submit annual and, when necessary, special reports to the General Assembly for its consideration.

Article 25

The Members of the United Nations agree to accept and carry out the decisions of the Security Council in accordance with the present Charter.

Article 26

In order to promote the establishment and maintenance of international peace and security with the least diversion for armaments of the world's human and economic resources, the Security Council shall be responsible for formulating, with the assistance of the Military Staff Committee referred to in Article 47, plans to be submitted to the Members of the United Nations for the establishment of a system for the regulation of armaments.

Voting

Article 27

1. Each member of the Security Council shall have one vote.

2. Decisions of the Security Council on procedural matters shall be made by an affirmative vote of seven members.

3. Decisions of the Security Council on all other matters shall be made by an affirmative vote of seven members, including the concurring votes of the permanent members; provided that, in decisions under Chapter VI, and under paragraph 3 of Article 52, a party to a dispute shall abstain from voting.

Procedure

Article 28

1. The Security Council shall be so organized as to be able to function continuously. Each member of the Security Council shall for this purpose be represented at all times at the seat of the Organization.

2. The Security Council shall hold periodic meetings at which each of its members may, if it so desires, be represented by a member of the government or by some other specially designated representative.

3. The Security Council may hold meetings at such places other than the seat of the Organization as in its judgment will best facilitate its work.

Article 29

The Security Council may establish such subsidiary organs as it deems necessary for the performance of its functions.

Article 30

The Security Council shall adopt its own rules of procedure, including the method of selecting its President.

Article 31

Any Member of the United Nations which is not a member of the Security Council may participate, without vote, in the discussion of any question brought before the Security Council whenever the latter considers that the interests of that Member are specially affected.

Article 32

Any Member of the United Nations which is not a member of the Security Council or any state which is not a Member of the United Nations, if it is a party to a dispute under consideration by the Security Council, shall be invited to participate, without vote, in the discussion relating to the dispute. The Security Council shall lay down such conditions as it deems just for the participation of a state which is not a Member of the United Nations.

CHAPTER VI

PACIFIC SETTLEMENT OF DISPUTES

Article 33

1. The parties to any dispute, the continuance of which is likely to endanger the maintenance of international peace and security, shall, first of all, seek a solution by negotiation, enquiry, mediation, conciliation, arbitration, judicial settlement, resort to regional agencies or arrangements, or other peaceful means of their own choice.
2. The Security Council shall, when it deems necessary, call upon the parties to settle their dispute by such means.

Article 34

The Security Council may investigate any dispute, or any situation which might lead to international friction or give rise to a dispute, in order to determine whether the continuance of the dispute or situation is likely to endanger the maintenance of international peace and security.

Article 35

1. Any Member of the United Nations may bring any dispute, or any situation of the nature referred to in Article 34,

to the attention of the Security Council or of the General Assembly.

2. A state which is not a Member of the United Nations may bring to the attention of the Security Council or of the General Assembly any dispute to which it is a party if it accepts in advance, for the purposes of the dispute, the obligations of pacific settlement provided in the present Charter.

3. The proceedings of the General Assembly in respect of matters brought to its attention under this Article will be subject to the provisions of Articles 11 and 12.

Article 36

1. The Security Council may, at any stage of a dispute of the nature referred to in Article 33 or of a situation of like nature, recommend appropriate procedures or methods of adjustment.

2. The Security Council should take into consideration any procedures for the settlement of the dispute which have already been adopted by the parties.

3. In making recommendations under this Article the Security Council should also take into consideration that legal disputes should as a general rule be referred by the parties to the International Court of Justice in accordance with the provisions of the Statute of the Court.

Article 37

1. Should the parties to a dispute of the nature referred to in Article 33 fail to settle it by the means indicated in that Article, they shall refer it to the Security Council.

2. If the Security Council deems that the continuance of the dispute is in fact likely to endanger the maintenance of international peace and security, it shall decide whether to take action under Article 36 or to recommend such terms of settlement as it may consider appropriate.

Article 38

Without prejudice to the provisions of Articles 33 to 37, the Security Council may, if all the parties to any dispute so request, make recommendations to the parties with a view to a pacific settlement of the dispute.

CHAPTER VII

ACTION WITH RESPECT TO THREATS TO THE
PEACE, BREACHES OF THE PEACE,
AND ACTS OF AGGRESSION

Article 39

The Security Council shall determine the existence of any threat to the peace, breach of the peace, or act of aggression and shall make recommendations, or decide what measures shall be taken in accordance with Articles 41 and 42, to maintain or restore international peace and security.

Article 40

In order to prevent an aggravation of the situation, the Security Council may, before making the recommendations or deciding upon the measures provided for in Article 39, call upon the parties concerned to comply with such provisional measures as it deems necessary or desirable. Such provisional measures shall be without prejudice to the rights, claims, or position of the parties concerned. The Security Council shall duly take account of failure to comply with such provisional measures.

Article 41

The Security Council may decide what measures not involving the use of armed force are to be employed to give effect to its decisions, and it may call upon the Members of the United Nations to apply such measures. These may include complete or partial interruption of economic relations and of rail, sea, air, postal, telegraphic, radio, and other means of communication, and the severance of diplomatic relations.

Article 42

Should the Security Council consider that measures provided for in Article 41 would be inadequate or have proved to be inadequate, it may take such action by air, sea, or land forces as may be necessary to maintain or restore international peace and security. Such action may include demonstrations, blockade, and other operations by air, sea, or land forces of Members of the United Nations.

Article 43

1. All Members of the United Nations, in order to contribute to the maintenance of international peace and security, undertake to make available to the Security Council, on its call and in accordance with a special agreement or agreements, armed forces, assistance and facilities, including rights of passage, necessary for the purpose of maintaining international peace and security.

2. Such agreement or agreements shall govern the numbers and types of forces, their degree of readiness and general location, and the nature of the facilities and assistance to be provided.

3. The agreement or agreements shall be negotiated as soon as possible on the initiative of the Security Council. They shall be concluded between the Security Council and Members or between the Security Council and groups of Members and shall be subject to ratification by the signatory states in accordance with their respective constitutional processes.

Article 44

When the Security Council has decided to use force it shall, before calling upon a Member not represented on it to provide armed forces in fulfilment of the obligations assumed under Article 43, invite that Member, if the Member so desires, to participate in the decisions of the Security Council concerning the employment of contingents of that Member's armed forces.

Article 45

In order to enable the United Nations to take urgent military measures, Members shall hold immediately available national air-force contingents for combined international enforcement action. The strength and degree of readiness of these contingents and plans for their combined action shall be determined, within the limits laid down in the special agreement or agreements referred to in Article 43, by the Security Council with the assistance of the Military Staff Committee.

Article 46

Plans for the application of armed force shall be made by the Security Council with the assistance of the Military Staff Committee.

Article 47

1. There shall be established a Military Staff Committee to advise and assist the Security Council on all questions relating to the Security Council's military requirements for the maintenance of international peace and security, the employment and command of forces placed at its disposal, the regulation of armaments, and possible disarmament.

2. The Military Staff Committee shall consist of the Chiefs of Staff of the permanent members of the Security Council or their representatives. Any Member of the United Nations not permanently represented on the Committee shall be invited by the Committee to be associated with it when the efficient discharge of the Committee's responsibilities requires the participation of that Member in its work.

3. The Military Staff Committee shall be responsible under the Security Council for the strategic direction of any armed forces placed at the disposal of the Security Council. Questions relating to the command of such forces shall be worked out subsequently.

4. The Military Staff Committee, with the authorization of the Security Council and after consultation with appropriate regional agencies, may establish regional subcommittees.

Article 48

1. The action required to carry out the decisions of the Security Council for the maintenance of international peace and security shall be taken by all the Members of the United Nations or by some of them, as the Security Council may determine.

2. Such decisions shall be carried out by the Members of the United Nations directly and through their action in the appropriate international agencies of which they are members.

Article 49

The Members of the United Nations shall join in affording

mutual assistance in carrying out the measures decided upon by the Security Council.

Article 50

If preventive or enforcement measures against any state are taken by the Security Council, any other state, whether a Member of the United Nations or not, which finds itself confronted with special economic problems arising from the carrying out of those measures shall have the right to consult the Security Council with regard to a solution of those problems.

Article 51

Nothing in the present Charter shall impair the inherent right of individual or collective self-defense if an armed attack occurs against a Member of the United Nations, until the Security Council has taken measures necessary to maintain international peace and security. Measures taken by Members in the exercise of this right of self-defense shall be immediately reported to the Security Council and shall not in any way affect the authority and responsibility of the Security Council under the present Charter to take at any time such action as it deems necessary in order to maintain or restore international peace and security.

CHAPTER VIII

REGIONAL ARRANGEMENTS

Article 52

1. Nothing in the present Charter precludes the existence of regional arrangements or agencies for dealing with such matters relating to the maintenance of international peace and security as are appropriate for regional action, provided that such arrangements or agencies and their activities are consistent with the Purposes and Principles of the United Nations.

2. The Members of the United Nations entering into such arrangements or constituting such agencies shall make every effort to achieve pacific settlement of local disputes through such regional arrangements or by such regional agencies before referring them to the Security Council.

3. The Security Council shall encourage the development of pacific settlement of local disputes through such regional

arrangements or by such regional agencies either on the initiative of the states concerned or by reference from the Security Council.

4. This Article in no way impairs the application of Articles 34 and 35.

Article 53

1. The Security Council shall, where appropriate, utilize such regional arrangements or agencies for enforcement action under its authority. But no enforcement action shall be taken under regional arrangements or by regional agencies without the authorization of the Security Council, with the exception of measures against any enemy state, as defined in paragraph 2 of this Article, provided for pursuant to Article 107 or in regional arrangements directed against renewal of aggressive policy on the part of any such state, until such time as the Organization may, on request of the Governments concerned, be charged with the responsibility for preventing further aggression by such a state.

2. The term enemy state as used in paragraph 1 of this Article applies to any state which during the Second World War has been an enemy of any signatory of the present Charter.

Article 54

The Security Council shall at all times be kept fully informed of activities undertaken or in contemplation under regional arrangements or by regional agencies for the maintenance of international peace and security.

CHAPTER IX

INTERNATIONAL ECONOMIC AND SOCIAL COOPERATION

Article 55

With a view to the creation of conditions of stability and well-being which are necessary for peaceful and friendly relations among nations based on respect for the principle of equal rights and self-determination of peoples, the United Nations shall promote:

a. higher standards of living, full employment, and conditions of economic and social progress and development;

b. solutions of international economic, social, health, and related problems; and international cultural and educational cooperation; and

c. universal respect for, and observance of, human rights and fundamental freedoms for all without distinction as to race, sex, language, or religion.

Article 56

All Members pledge themselves to take joint and separate action in cooperation with the Organization for the achievement of the purposes set forth in Article 55.

Article 57

1. The various specialized agencies, established by intergovernmental agreement and having wide international responsibilities, as defined in their basic instruments, in economic, social, cultural, educational, health, and related fields, shall be brought into relationship with the United Nations in accordance with the provisions of Article 63.

2. Such agencies thus brought into relationship with the United Nations are hereinafter referred to as specialized agencies.

Article 58

The Organization shall make recommendations for the coordination of the policies and activities of the specialized agencies.

Article 59

The Organization shall, where appropriate, initiate negotiations among the states concerned for the creation of any new specialized agencies required for the accomplishment of the purposes set forth in Article 55.

Article 60

Responsibility for the discharge of the functions of the Organization set forth in this Chapter shall be vested in the General Assembly and, under the authority of the General Assembly, in the Economic and Social Council, which shall have for this purpose the powers set forth in Chapter X.

CHAPTER X

THE ECONOMIC AND SOCIAL COUNCIL

Composition
Article 61

1. The Economic and Social Council shall consist of eighteen Members of the United Nations elected by the General Assembly.

2. Subject to the provisions of paragraph 3, six members of the Economic and Social Council shall be elected each year for a term of three years. A retiring member shall be eligible for immediate re-election.

3. At the first election, eighteen members of the Economic and Social Council shall be chosen. The term of office of six members so chosen shall expire at the end of one year, and of six other members at the end of two years, in accordance with arrangements made by the General Assembly.

4. Each member of the Economic and Social Council shall have one representative.

Functions and Powers
Article 62

1. The Economic and Social Council may make or initiate studies and reports with respect to international economic, social, cultural, educational, health, and related matters and may make recommendations with respect to any such matters to the General Assembly, to the Members of the United Nations, and to the specialized agencies concerned.

2. It may make recommendations for the purpose of promoting respect for, and observance of, human rights and fundamental freedoms for all.

3. It may prepare draft conventions for submission to the General Assembly, with respect to matters falling within its competence.

4. It may call, in accordance with the rules prescribed by the United Nations, international conferences on matters falling within its competence.

Article 63

1. The Economic and Social Council may enter into agreements with any of the agencies referred to in Article 57, defining the terms on which the agency concerned shall be

brought into relationship with the United Nations. Such agreements shall be subject to approval by the General Assembly.

2. It may coordinate the activities of the specialized agencies through consultation with and recommendations to such agencies and through recommendations to the General Assembly and to the Members of the United Nations.

Article 64

1. The Economic and Social Council may take appropriate steps to obtain regular reports from the specialized agencies. It may make arrangements with the Members of the United Nations and with the specialized agencies to obtain reports on the steps taken to give effect to its own recommendations and to recommendations on matters falling within its competence made by the General Assembly.

2. It may communicate its observations on these reports to the General Assembly.

Article 65

The Economic and Social Council may furnish information to the Security Council and shall assist the Security Council upon its request.

Article 66

1. The Economic and Social Council shall perform such functions as fall within its competence in connection with the carrying out of the recommendations of the General Assembly.

2. It may, with the approval of the General Assembly, perform services at the request of Members of the United Nations and at the request of specialized agencies.

3. It shall perform such other functions as are specified elsewhere in the present Charter or as may be assigned to it by the General Assembly.

Voting

Article 67

1. Each member of the Economic and Social Council shall have one vote.

2. Decisions of the Economic and Social Council shall be made by a majority of the members present and voting.

Procedure

Article 68

The Economic and Social Council shall set up commissions in economic and social fields and for the promotion of human rights, and such other commissions as may be required for the performance of its functions.

Article 69

The Economic and Social Council shall invite any Member of the United Nations to participate, without vote, in its deliberations on any matter of particular concern to that Member.

Article 70

The Economic and Social Council may make arrangements for representatives of the specialized agencies to participate, without vote, in its deliberations and in those of the commissions established by it, and for its representatives to participate in the deliberations of the specialized agencies.

Article 71

The Economic and Social Council may make suitable arrangements for consultation with non-governmental organizations which are concerned with matters within its competence. Such arrangements may be made with international organizations and, where appropriate, with national organizations after consultation with the Member of the United Nations concerned.

Article 72

1. The Economic and Social Council shall adopt its own rules of procedure, including the method of selecting its President.

2. The Economic and Social Council shall meet as required in accordance with its rules, which shall include provision for the convening of meetings on the request of a majority of its members.

CHAPTER XI

DECLARATION REGARDING
NON-SELF-GOVERNING TERRITORIES

Article 73

Members of the United Nations which have or assume responsibilities for the administration of territories whose peoples have not yet attained a full measure of self-government recognize the principle that the interests of the inhabitants of these territories are paramount, and accept as a sacred trust the obligation to promote to the utmost, within the system of international peace and security established by the present Charter, the well-being of the inhabitants of these territories, and, to this end:

a. to ensure, with due respect for the culture of the peoples concerned, their political, economic, social, and educational advancement, their just treatment, and their protection against abuses;

b. to develop self-government, to take due account of the political aspirations of the peoples, and to assist them in the progressive development of their free political institutions, according to the particular circumstances of each territory and its peoples and their varying stages of advancement;

c. to further international peace and security;

d. to promote constructive measures of development, to encourage research, and to cooperate with one another and, when and where appropriate, with specialized international bodies with a view to the practical achievement of the social, economic, and scientific purposes set forth in this Article; and

e. to transmit regularly to the Secretary-General for information purposes, subject to such limitation as security and constitutional considerations may require, statistical and other information of a technical nature relating to economic, social, and educational conditions in the territories for which they are respectively responsible other than those territories to which Chapters XII and XIII apply.

Article 74

Members of the United Nations also agree that their policy in respect of the territories to which this Chapter applies, no less than in respect of their metropolitan areas, must be based on the general principle of good-neighborliness, due account being taken of the interests and well-being of the rest of the world, in social, economic, and commercial matters.

CHAPTER XII

INTERNATIONAL TRUSTEESHIP SYSTEM

Article 75

The United Nations shall establish under its authority an international trusteeship system for the administration and supervision of such territories as may be placed thereunder by subsequent individual agreements. These territories are hereinafter referred to as trust territories.

Article 76

The basic objectives of the trusteeship system, in accordance with the Purposes of the United Nations laid down in Article 1 of the present Charter, shall be:

    a. to further international peace and security;

    b. to promote the political, economic, social, and educational advancement of the inhabitants of the trust territories, and their progressive development towards self-government or independence as may be appropriate to the particular circumstances of each territory and its peoples and the freely expressed wishes of the peoples concerned, and as may be provided by the terms of each trusteeship agreement;

    c. to encourage respect for human rights and for fundamental freedoms for all without distinction as to race, sex, language, or religion, and to encourage recognition of the interdependence of the peoples of the world; and

    d. to ensure equal treatment in social, economic, and commercial matters for all Members of the United Nations and their nationals, and also equal treatment for the latter in the administration of justice, without prejudice to the attainment of the foregoing objectives and subject to the provisions of Article 80.

Article 77

1. The trusteeship system shall apply to such territories in the following categories as may be placed thereunder by means of trusteeship agreements:

    a. territories now held under mandate;

    b. territories which may be detached from enemy states as a result of the Second World War; and

c. territories voluntarily placed under the system by states responsible for their administration.

2. It will be a matter for subsequent agreement as to which territories in the foregoing categories will be brought under the trusteeship system and upon what terms.

Article 78

The trusteeship system shall not apply to territories which have become Members of the United Nations, relationship among which shall be based on respect for the principle of sovereign equality.

Article 79

The terms of trusteeship for each territory to be placed under the trusteeship system, including any alteration or amendment, shall be agreed upon by the states directly concerned, including the mandatory power in the case of territories held under mandate by a Member of the United Nations, and shall be approved as provided for in Articles 83 and 85.

Article 80

1. Except as may be agreed upon in individual trusteeship agreements, made under Articles 77, 79, and 81, placing each territory under the trusteeship system, and until such agreements have been concluded, nothing in this Chapter shall be constructed in or of itself to alter in any manner the rights whatsoever of any states or any peoples or the terms of existing international instruments to which Members of the United Nations may respectively be parties.

2. Paragraph 1 of this Article shall not be interpreted as giving grounds for delay or postponement of the negotiation and conclusion of agreements for placing mandated and other territories under the trusteeship system as provided for in Article 77.

Article 81

The trusteeship agreement shall in each case include the terms under which the trust territory will be administered and designate the authority which will exercise the administration of the trust territory. Such authority, hereinafter called the administering authority, may be one or more states or the Organization itself.

Article 82

There may be designated, in any trusteeship agreement, a strategic area or areas which may include part or all of the trust territory to which the agreement applies, without prejudice to any special agreement or agreements made under Article 43.

Article 83

1. All functions of the United Nations relating to strategic areas, including the approval of the terms of the trusteeship agreements and of their alteration or amendment, shall be exercised by the Security Council.

2. The basic objectives set forth in Article 76 shall be applicable to the people of each strategic area.

3. The Security Council shall, subject to the provisions of the trusteeship agreements and without prejudice to security considerations, avail itself of the assistance of the Trusteeship Council to perform those functions of the United Nations under the trusteeship system relating to political, economic, social, and educational matters in the strategic areas.

Article 84

It shall be the duty of the administering authority to ensure that the trust territory shall play its part in the maintenance of international peace and security. To this end the administering authority may make use of volunteer forces, facilities, and assistance from the trust territory in carrying out the obligations towards the Security Council undertaken in this regard by the administering authority, as well as for local defense and the maintenance of law and order within the trust territory.

Article 85

1. The functions of the United Nations with regard to trusteeship agreements for all areas not designated as strategic, including the approval of the terms of the trusteeship agreements and of their alteration or amendment, shall be exercised by the General Assembly.

2. The Trusteeship Council, operating under the authority

of the General Assembly, shall assist the General Assembly in carrying out these functions.

CHAPTER XIII

THE TRUSTEESHIP COUNCIL

Composition

Article 86

1. The Trusteeship Council shall consist of the following Members of the United Nations:

    a. those Members administering trust territories;

    b. such of those Members mentioned by name in Article 23 as are not administering trust territories; and

    c. as many other Members elected for three-year terms by the General Assembly as may be necessary to ensure that the total number of members of the Trusteeship Council is equally divided between those Members of the United Nations which administer trust territories and those which do not.

2. Each member of the Trusteeship Council shall designate one specially qualified person to represent it therein.

Functions and Powers

Article 87

The General Assembly and, under its authority, the Trusteeship Council, in carrying out their functions, may:

    a. consider reports submitted by the administering authority;

    b. accept petitions and examine them in consultation with the administering authority;

    c. provide for periodic visits to the respective trust territories at times agreed upon with the administering authority; and

    d. take these and other actions in conformity with the terms of the trusteeship agreements.

Article 88

The Trusteeship Council shall formulate a questionnaire

on the political, economic, social, and educational advancement of the inhabitants of each trust territory, and the administering authority for each trust territory, within the
competence of the General Assembly shall make an annual
report to the General Assembly upon the basis of such
questionnaire.

Voting

Article 89

1. Each member of the Trusteeship Council shall have
one vote.
2. Decisions of the Trusteeship Council shall be made by
a majority of the members present and voting.

Procedure

Article 90

1. The Trusteeship Council shall adopt its own rules of
procedure, including the method of selecting its President.
2. The Trusteeship Council shall meet as required in accordance with its rules, which shall include provision for the
convening of meetings on the request of a majority of its
members.

Article 91

The Trusteeship Council shall, when appropriate, avail itself of the assistance of the Economic and Social Council
and of the specialized agencies in regard to matters with
which they are respectively concerned.

CHAPTER XIV

THE INTERNATIONAL COURT OF JUSTICE

Article 92

The International Court of Justice shall be the principal
judicial organ of the United Nations. It shall function in accordance with the annexed Statute, which is based upon the
Statute of the Permanent Court of International Justice and
forms an integral part of the present Charter.

Article 93

1. All Members of the United Nations are *ipso facto* parties to the Statute of the International Court of Justice.

2. A state which is not a Member of the United Nations may become a party to the Statute of the International Court of Justice on conditions to be determined in each case by the General Assembly upon the recommendation of the Security Council.

Article 94

1. Each Member of the United Nations undertakes to comply with the decision of the International Court of Justice in any case to which it is a party.

2. If any party to a case fails to perform the obligations incumbent upon it under a judgment rendered by the Court, the other party may have recourse to the Security Council, which may, if it deems necessary, make recommendations or decide upon measures to be taken to give effect to the judgment.

Article 95

Nothing in the present Charter shall prevent Members of the United Nations from entrusting the solution of their differences to other tribunals by virtue of agreements already in existence or which may be concluded in the future.

Article 96

1. The General Assembly or the Security Council may request the International Court of Justice to give an advisory opinion on any legal question.

2. Other organs of the United Nations and specialized agencies, which may at any time be so authorized by the General Assembly, may also request advisory opinions of the Court on legal questions arising within the scope of their activities.

CHAPTER XV

THE SECRETARIAT

Article 97

The Secretariat shall comprise a Secretary-General and such staff as the Organization may require. The Secretary-

General shall be appointed by the General Assembly upon the recommendation of the Security Council. He shall be the chief administrative officer of the Organization.

Article 98

The Secretary-General shall act in that capacity in all meetings of the General Assembly, of the Security Council, of the Economic and Social Council, and of the Trusteeship Council, and shall perform such other functions as are entrusted to him by these organs. The Secretary-General shall make an annual report to the General Assembly on the work of the Organization.

Article 99

The Secretary-General may bring to the attention of the Security Council any matter which in his opinion may threaten the maintenance of international peace and security.

Article 100

1. In the performance of their duties, the Secretary-General and the staff shall not seek or receive instructions from any government or from any other authority external to the Organization. They shall refrain from any action which might reflect on their position as international officials responsible only to the Organization.

2. Each Member of the United Nations undertakes to respect the exclusively international character of the responsibilities of the Secretary-General and the staff and not to seek to influence them in the discharge of their responsibilities.

Article 101

1. The staff shall be appointed by the Secretary-General under regulations established by the General Assembly.

2. Appropriate staffs shall be permanently assigned to the Economic and Social Council, the Trusteeship Council, and, as required, to other organs of the United Nations. These staffs shall form a part of the Secretariat.

3. The paramount consideration in the employment of the staff and in the determination of the conditions of service shall be the necessity of securing the highest standards of efficiency, competence, and integrity. Due regard shall be

paid to the importance of recruiting the staff on as wide a geographical basis as possible.

CHAPTER XVI

MISCELLANEOUS PROVISIONS

Article 102

1. Every treaty and every international agreement entered into by any Member of the United Nations after the present Charter comes into force shall as soon as possible be registered with the Secretariat and published by it.

2. No party to any such treaty or international agreement which has not been registered in accordance with the provisions of paragraph 1 of this Article may invoke that treaty or agreement before any organ of the United Nations.

Article 103

In the event of a conflict between the obligations of the Members of the United Nations under the present Charter and their obligations under any other international agreement, their obligations under the present Charter shall prevail.

Article 104

The Organization shall enjoy in the territory of each of its Members such legal capacity as may be necessary for the exercise of its functions and the fulfilment of its purposes.

Article 105

1. The Organization shall enjoy in the territory of each of its Members such privileges and immunities as are necessary for the fulfilment of its purposes.

2. Representatives of the Members of the United Nations and officials of the Organization shall similarly enjoy such privileges and immunities as are necessary for the independent exercise of their functions in connection with the Organization.

3. The General Assembly may make recommendations with a view to determining the details of the application of paragraphs 1 and 2 of this Article or may propose conventions to the Members of the United Nations for this purpose.

CHAPTER XVII

TRANSITIONAL SECURITY ARRANGEMENTS

Article 106

Pending the coming into force of such special agreements referred to in Article 43 as in the opinion of the Security Council enable it to begin the exercise of its responsibilities under Article 42, the parties to the Four-Nation Declaration, signed at Moscow, October 30, 1943, and France, shall, in accordance with the provisions of paragraph 5 of that Declaration, consult with one another and as occasion requires with other Members of the United Nations with a view to such joint action on behalf of the Organization as may be necessary for the purpose of maintaining international peace and security.

Article 107

Nothing in the present Charter shall invalidate or preclude action, in relation to any state which during the Second World War has been an enemy of any signatory to the present Charter, taken or authorized as a result of that war by the Governments having responsibility for such action.

CHAPTER XVIII

AMENDMENTS

Article 108

Amendments to the present Charter shall come into force for all Members of the United Nations when they have been adopted by a vote of two thirds of the members of the General Assembly and ratified in accordance with their respective constitutional processes by two thirds of the Members of the United Nations, including all the permanent members of the Security Council.

Article 109

1. A general conference of the Members of the United Nations for the purpose of reviewing the present Charter may be held at a date and place to be fixed by a two-thirds vote of the members of the General Assembly and by a vote of any

seven members of the Security Council. Each Member of the United Nations shall have one vote in the conference.

2. Any alteration of the present Charter recommended by a two-thirds vote of the conference shall take effect when ratified in accordance with their respective constitutional processes by two thirds of the Members of the United Nations, including all the permanent members of the Security Council.

3. If such a conference has not been held before the tenth annual session of the General Assembly following the coming into force of the present Charter, the proposal to call such a conference shall be placed on the agenda of that session of the General Assembly, and the conference shall be held if so decided by a majority vote of the members of the General Assembly and by a vote of any seven members of the Security Council.

CHAPTER XIX

RATIFICATION AND SIGNATURE

Article 110

1. The present Charter shall be ratified by the signatory states in accordance with their respective constitutional processes.

2. The ratifications shall be deposited with the Government of the United States of America, which shall notify all the signatory states of each deposit as well as the Secretary-General of the Organization when he has been appointed.

3. The present Charter shall come into force upon the deposit of ratifications by the Republic of China, France, the Union of Soviet Socialist Republics, the United Kingdom of Great Britain and Northern Ireland, and the United States of America, and by a majority of the other signatory states. A protocol of the ratifications deposited shall thereupon be drawn up by the Government of the United States of America, which shall communicate copies thereof to all the signatory states.

4. The states signatory to the present Charter which ratify it after it has come into force will become original Members of the United Nations on the date of the deposit of their respective ratifications.

Article 111

The present Charter, of which the Chinese, French, Russian, English, and Spanish texts are equally authentic, shall remain deposited in the archives of the Government of the United States of America. Duly certified copies thereof shall be transmitted by that Government to the Governments of the other signatory states.

IN FAITH WHEREOF the representatives of the Governments of the United Nations have signed the present Charter.

DONE at the city of San Francisco the twenty-sixth day of June, one thousand nine hundred and forty-five.

Note: The Statute of the International Court of Justice is an integral part of the Charter of the United Nations. It has been omitted here, however, since, in a book of this size, space for appended material is limited.

APPENDIX C

*The eighty-two member states of the United Nations are:

Afghanistan	*France	*New Zealand
Albania,	Ghana	*Nicaragua,
*Argentina	Guinea	*Norway
*Australia	*Greece	Pakistan
Austria,	*Guatemala	*Panama
*Belgium	*Haiti	*Paraguay
*Bolivia,	*Honduras	*Peru
*Brazil	Hungary	*Philippines
Bulgaria	Iceland	*Poland
Burma,	*India,	Portugal
*Byelorussian SSR	Indonesia	Romania
Cambodia,	*Iran	*Saudi Arabia
*Canada	*Iraq	Spain
Ceylon	Ireland	Sudan
*Chile	Israel	Sweden
*China,	Italy	Thailand
*Colombia	Japan	Tunisia
*Costa Rica	Jordan	*Turkey
*Cuba	Laos	*Ukrainian SSR
*Czechoslovakia	*Lebanon	*Union of South Africa
*Denmark	*Liberia	*USSR
*Dominican Republic	Libya	**United Arab Republic
*Ecuador	*Luxembourg	*United Kingdom
*El Salvador	*Mexico	*United States
*Ethiopia	Morocco	*Uruguay
Federation of Malaya	Nepal	*Venezuela
Finland	*Netherlands	Yemen
		*Yugoslavia

*At the time the book went to press (November, 1960), the following additional seventeen states had just been admitted to membership in the United Nations: Cameroun, Central African Republic, Chad, Congo (Brazzaville), Congo (Leopoldville), Cyprus, Dahomey, Gabon, Ivory Coast, Madagascar, Mali,

Niger, Nigeria, Senegal, Somalia, Togo, Upper Volta. (The Islamic Republic of Mauritania is scheduled for independence November 28, 1960 and will probably apply for UN membership shortly thereafter.)

---

* Original member. ** In 1958, Egypt and Syria, original members of the United Nations, were united in a single state, the United Arab Republic.

INDEX